ENERGY
HEALING

ANN MARIE CHIASSON, MD

ENERGY
HEALING

The ESSENTIALS *of* SELF-CARE

 sounds true

Sounds True, Inc.
Boulder, CO 80306

This work is solely for personal growth and education. It should not be treated as a substitute for professional assistance, therapeutic activities such as psychotherapy or counseling, or medical advice. In the event of physical or mental distress, please consult with appropriate health professionals. The application of protocols and information in this book is the choice of each reader, who assumes full responsibility for his or her understandings, interpretations, and results. The author and publisher assume no responsibility for the actions or choices of any reader.

Cover and book design by Lisa Kerans
Illustrations and photos © by Sounds True

Quotes from Lalla, *Naked Song*, Coleman Barks, translator (Varanasi, India: Pilgrims Publishing, 2004) are reprinted with permission from Coleman Barks.

Printed in the United States of America

ISBN 978-1-60407-892-3

DEDICATION

One day during the process of writing this book, I hit a stumbling block in the creative process and the allocation of my time. There were so many important things in my life, including a very ill friend, tugging at me for time and attention. I sent out a petition to the energy field: "I must tend to those in need of healing and to those I love and care for. If you, the energy field, want this book written, can you send me some help with finishing this manuscript?"

A few days later, my mother called me and said, "I was thinking of coming out to visit for almost six weeks now. Would that be OK?"

OK? Yes! Here was the help!

My mother is my friend, my confidant, and also an editor. She helped me focus and assisted with the loving caretaking of my family during this journey. Her help arrived, and here is this book—from me, and my mother, to you.

I gratefully dedicate this book to my mother, Ernestine Marie Sadotti Smith.

I also dedicate this book to the fourteenth-century poetess Lalla and to the skilled and soulful poet Coleman Barks. Lalla's simple and profound poetry speaks to the awakened field of energy and to the mystery of life. Mr. Barks devotedly translated Lalla's poetry and brought it into my life through a book of her poems called *Naked Song*.

CONTENTS

THE ENERGY PRACTICES

In the years that I have been investigating physiological and emotional well-being, I have both observed and experienced the profound effects of energy healing. As more and more people are seeking ways to protect and enhance their own health, interest and awareness have grown concerning healing systems that address the subtle energies of the body and the environment. At the same time, the range of energy healing modalities available has vastly expanded—so much so that it can be very difficult to determine which one is best for you at any given moment. Not only may some of them seem odd, but you may feel that various systems appear to contradict each other.

We are very fortunate to have this new book by Dr. Ann Marie Chiasson to help us. She transcends the contradictions of multiple systems by focusing on their common root: the body itself. It is surprising how easily we can lose sight of the fact that everything we know about the health of the body has come into our awareness because of very close attention paid to the body in the first place. Systems of healing are constructed from observations, but they are always provisional, their efficacy always dependent upon ongoing revelations from the body. If you get stuck in the paradigm of a particular system, you may be blind to experiences that fall outside the parameters of that system. In these pages, Dr. Chiasson draws on her vast professional and personal expertise to connect us to the wisdom of the body itself.

I have had the privelege of knowing Dr. Chiasson as a student as well as a colleague at the Arizona Center for Integrative Medicine. She came to our center initially as a family physician and enrolled in the fellowship in Integrative Medicine. Upon graduation from that training, she joined our faculty as an assistant clinical professor of medicine, in charge of introducing medicine of the future to the medical students and residents who come to us. Her specialty interests are energy healing, meditation, and healing ceremony.

Professional and academic credentials do not fully convey all that Dr. Chiasson offers. I know her to be a doctor of tremendous compassion, vivacity, and good humor. She approaches healing with a spirit of reverent joy and incisive inquiry. Drawing upon years of personal exploration of healing traditions in North and South America, she continues to deepen her understanding of the mysteries of healing and the human experience. Furthermore, she is a wonderful storyteller who delights in the spontaneous discoveries that can occur in the midst of simple human interaction. It is not uncommon to walk away from a talk by Dr. Chiasson feeling like you've just had a laugh with a good friend, only to realize later how much you've learned.

As I continue to teach and refine Integrative Medicine, I remain firmly enthusiastic about the work of practioners like Dr. Ann Marie Chiasson. Not only is she deepening our awareness of the possibilities of energy healing, she is empowering individuals with the means to listen to the deep wisdom of their own bodies. She is also adept at discussing the interface of energy healing with conventional medicine. I consider this book an excellent guide for anyone interested in exploring energy as a means of maintaining healthy, dynamic living.

Health and Healing:
A Crucial Shift for Our Time

Forgetful one, get up!
It's dawn, time to start searching

—Lalla, *Naked Song*

This book is an induction into self-healing and into a heightened perception of energy within your body and, by extension, the world around you. You will learn energy practices that are helpful, and more fundamentally, you will learn to read reality from the level of energy. By reading reality at this level, you can drop into multiple layers of body information through what you sense, feel, see, and even hear about energy, and you can become adept at moving energy in your body and in your environment.

I began to learn energy healing before I even conceived that I might go to medical school. I had met a hands-on healer and took her energy healing class. I began to practice energy healing in my spare time. Years later, when I entered medical school, I was curious about how the energetic body interacted with the physical body and how the paradigm of energy healing would fit into what I would learn in conventional medicine. How would these two systems work together? From my perspective, one paradigm was not more valuable than the other; they seemed to be different views of the same theme: health and healing. Much to my surprise, none of the healers or physicians I encountered shared my view, nor do most of them now.

In addition, I had a medical condition that was causing chronic pain. While I was in residency, I had surgery for the problem, but the pain persisted even though there was no longer a medical reason for it. My doctor hinted that depression was the underlying cause. I knew that there was another paradigm that explained the pain and could lead me out of it. I knew from energy healing that the residual pain was located at the level of the energy body. I began to deepen my study of energy healing, visiting healers and shamans from around the world. By the time I was finally pain free, I had become hooked on what energy healers were teaching me.

Through this healing process I came to realize that our current approach to energy healing, energy modalities, and other healing paradigms (including conventional medicine) is too fractured. We focus on how to do techniques. We focus on the differences, or divergences, between the healing paradigms. We focus on how to eradicate our illness rather than on supporting the body's underlying healing mechanism. While this approach has brought many wonderful advances in the last two hundred years, to make the next leap in our experience of healing, we must go much deeper, to the common root of all our healing paradigms.

The one thing all the healing modalities have in common, at the deepest layer, is *the body*—at both the physical and energetic level. While this may seem obvious, the implications are profound. Just a few of these implications include:

- The body has its own awareness, which is quite distinct from the awareness we usually identify with.

- The body is self-healing and constantly moving toward self-healing.

- Rather than being the enemy, illness is a body-initiated move into healing.

- All the healing paradigms we know converge and are accessible to us at the level of the wisdom of the energy body.

The body is the source of the wisdom and information, but how do we harvest this knowledge? We learn to read reality and the body from the level of energy. Once we can begin to read reality at this level, all the different paradigms begin to make sense in a larger, fuller perspective. The different forms of healing begin to partner with each other with ease. Healing is no longer about using one technique for one problem and another technique for another; it is about learning how to read our own body to get the help we need to bring it back into balance.

I call this *body-mind medicine*. The body informs the mind of what is happening. We use the body as our tool, and the mind can formulate the questions and answers from the information the body provides. When we hold this "body-full" awareness from the reality of energy, healing becomes easier to explore and follow. Allowing the body to inform the mind is a natural process, yet through the shift over the past hundreds of years into developing our rational mind and rational processes, some of the connections from the body into the mind, and between the right and left hemispheres of the brain, have been dampened or overridden. This body-mind perspective is about opening the aperture of our awareness to allow more information from the energy body to come into play in our lives, in how we view our world (which informs our reality), and in healing.

In this book, I will discuss the reality of energy by exploring the *unified field* and the *shamanic field*. It is through this exploration that the convergence happens. Reading or seeing reality from the level of energy is not learning the notes to a song; it is learning what the music is and how to make the music. Many people have asked me whether I "believe in" energy healing. I want to stress that learning and using energy healing is not about belief. I do not have to believe in electricity for the lights in my house to turn on. Nature lives by the rules of energy. We do too, although we are not always aware of it, and some of us are rarely aware of it. When I was pregnant with my first child, I was in awe that while I was working in the hospital, going grocery shopping, or sleeping, the fetus inside my body was growing. My awareness of the pregnancy had little role; the baby was growing whether or not I was paying attention. In the same way, our bodies are living in, aware of, and using energy even when we're not conscious of it doing so. Energy healing is about opening the aperture of how we see, feel, and experience the world. Energy moves in the body and in our environment all the time. We each have a natural ability to read it and work with it, although individual skillfulness varies.

I will induct you into this radically different way of reading your reality by introducing both structured and unstructured information. We need structured information to build the scaffolding of a new topic being learned. We also need unstructured information, such as experience, to make the information come alive and shift into knowledge. Add years of knowledge with more experience, and one tumbles into wisdom. Experience is the best form of unstructured information, so I encourage you to do the exercises in this book until you are adept at each one. Training in energy healing from this perspective takes time. I encourage you to give yourself nine months before you look back to assess what has shifted in your health, healing, and life.

I will introduce you to multiple paradigms of energy healing so you can begin to see what is underlying the energy perspective. You can use the one that suits you best or explore all the paradigms. It does not matter how you view energy healing at first. It only matters that you continue to explore what is happening in your body. This is how you will be able to harvest what is happening from the level of energy for yourself.

I also use multiple stories to convey information or my experience of becoming aware of certain aspects of energy healing. While these may seem like digressions, I include them to give you a map similar to an experience. Stories carry energy and pattern; it is the energy and pattern within the story that allows the listener or reader to glean a secondhand experience from the story. The map of energy and pattern is an experiential map that can be picked up through a story, often without effort. Providing this experiential map is the function of myth, stories, and more recently, movies, in cultures throughout the world. The pattern of an experience can be conferred through a story, as if one has had the experience itself. Even conventional medicine is now embracing the power of story in the healing process; this new aspect of medicine is called *narrative medicine.* In an effort to give you a better ability to read energy and pattern in the energy healing process, I include stories from my experiences at different stages of my own exploration.

We can also talk about structured and unstructured information as rational and nonrational information and even as right- and left-hemisphere brain activity. Rational thought and didactic learning occur mostly in the left hemisphere, and nonrational learning and nonrational abilities occur mostly in the right hemisphere. Energy healing and most of the skills used to sense, see, feel, and read energy are housed in the nonrational area of the brain. Reading reality from the level of energy involves skills that depend on the experiential, nonrational right side of the brain. If you have never worked with energy, then learning to read energy and to engage in energy healing are like learning to speak a foreign language. The more you strive or struggle to understand this material, the more you are using the rational process instead of the experiential process. You may understand the concepts immediately, yet if you don't, do not become concerned. Instead, I encourage you to let your world tilt, to use the practices, and to watch what happens. The book may bring up as many new questions as it does answers. If this happens, it means you are well on your way to learning this new language.

Expect to be shifted by what you learn. After you have used this book's techniques for a few months or longer, you may find that the way you view your body—as well as your life and the world around you—has changed. Likely, you will feel more a part of the natural world again. You will fall back into sync with the naturalness of what is going on within you and around you, and your sense of being separate from the natural world will disappear. The wisdom of the body is housed within the body. It is our access to this wisdom that governs how we work with the physical body and energy body. As you work with the practices in this book, I suggest you use the techniques rigorously just as they are described for a few months in order to harvest what each practice is offering. However, once you begin to experience the body at the level of energy, you may find variations or new practices that are offered up by the wisdom of your body.

I encourage you to allow your body and the energy within your body and the natural world around you to become your primary teachers and guides.

Ann Marie Chiasson, MD
Tucson, Arizona
January 2013

CHAPTER 1

The Basics of Energy Healing

Lost in the wilderness between
true awareness and the senses
I suddenly woke inside myself . . .

—Lalla, *Naked Song*

The underlying paradigm of energy was first documented five thousand years ago in India, in a text called the Upanishads,[1] and also in the original texts of traditional Chinese medicine (TCM).[2] Ninety-four cultures have been documented as having a concept that describes the underlying energy of the body.[3] Each of these cultures has a model or system of healing based on an underlying energy flow, and there are both similarities and differences in how they describe and map out the energy. I will give you a unified view of a few of these various systems, so you can see how they are inter-related, as I do.

Energy medicine was commonly used in the West as late as the 1800s, most notably by Franz Mesmer, a nineteenth-century physician who was the father of hypnosis (and whose name is the root of the word *mesmerize*).[4] Mesmer wrote about animal magnetism, an energy that could be transferred between objects, and he practiced energy transference. The concept of an underlying energy or vital force was part of conventional medicine until the late nineteenth century, when medical educators and physicians began to delineate the body and its illnesses by organ systems (such as cardiac disease, respiratory disease, and bone disease).[5]

While this delineation fostered wonderful advancements, we are now seeing a reintroduction or resurgence of energy healing techniques in Western culture and medicine. We are now in an integration phase; we are able to harvest the wisdoms of other paradigms of healing and integrate them into our current views and therapies. We see that medicine is an art and that many of these older paradigms— including energy healing, traditional Chinese medicine, ayurvedic medicine, mind-body medicine (which dates back to the ancient Greek temples of Asclepius), and herbal or botanical medicine—are of value in treating certain illnesses. Energy therapies and techniques can help with disease prevention and general wellness—and with conditions where conventional medicine is insufficient, such as chronic pain, chronic disease, and healing from deep psychological or physical trauma. We are beginning to see an integration of many different paradigms and can explore which technique works best for which disease or combination of symptoms.

Today, the United States' National Center for Complementary and Alternative Medicine (NCCAM), part of the National Institutes of Health (NIH), delineates two types of energy fields: *veritable* (measured) and *putative* (yet to be measured). Veritable energy fields are scientifically measurable; these include, NCCAM notes, "electromagnetic fields used in magnetic resonance imaging, cardiac pacemakers, radiation therapy, ultraviolet light for psoriasis, and laser keratoplasty."[6] Even though these therapies use energy fields, conventional medicine does not refer to techniques that work with veritable energy fields as *energy medicine* or *energy healing*. Instead, these terms are currently applied to healing techniques that fall within the putative fields that NCCAM describes. According to NCCAM, putative fields "have defied measurement to date by reproducible methods."[7] However, NCCAM recognizes that the concept of people being infused with a subtle form of energy has persisted for more than two thousand years and that this energy has many names, "such as *qi* in traditional Chinese medicine (TCM), *ki* in the Japanese *kampo* system, *doshas* in ayurvedic medicine, and elsewhere as *prana, etheric energy, fohat, orgone, odic force, mana,* and *homeopathic resonance.*"[8]

NCCAM currently defines energy healing as those complementary and alternative medicine techniques that involve the putative fields. Both within and outside conventional medicine circles, conversations about energy and working with the energy field of the body are under way, even though some physicians and scientists consider this energy body and energy healing to be "hocus pocus." What *I* can share is that many, or even the majority, of physicians who have practiced for many years intuitively understand the role of something other than science in healing. We just do not have a common language for what this "other" thing is at the moment.

Lack of medical research on and scientific verification of the body's energy field has kept many conventional medical practitioners and researchers from accepting and using energy healing techniques. It is difficult to research the energy field of the body, although some research is appearing. There is reproducible, fair data showing that energy healing can decrease pain and the use of pain medication. We can also measure the effect an energy healer has on plants and animals.[9] Ambiguities in the definition of energy healing and what it is useful for will likely continue until a method is devised to measure accurately the body's energy field in a way that jibes with conventional medicine.[10] There is early work in measuring the body's energy field by researchers in the United States, Canada, and Europe, including James Oschman, PhD, Melinda Connor, PhD, and Gary Schwartz, PhD.

THE ENERGY BODY

Energy healing, or energy medicine, is based on the ancient concept that there is a vital force, an underlying flow of energy, both within the physical body and extending from it. The body's entire energy system is referred to as *the energy field, the energy body, the biofield,* or *the subtle body*—all interchangeable terms. This system of energy is the template from which the physical body grows, and it guides the body's function. I like to think of the physical body as a plant and the energy body as the soil in which the plant grows. The soil affects the plant's growth and health. While factors other than the soil (such as trauma, freezing temperatures, or poor sunlight) might impact the health of the plant, the overall homeostasis and growth of the plant relies on the soil.

The flow of energy through the subtle body can be compared to the flow of water through a river and its tributaries. If a dam is built along the river (an energy block forms) or a huge rain dumps extra water into the river (there is an enormous influx of energy), the water will overflow to create new streams. If there is a paucity of water (energy), the smaller, shallower tributaries will dry up. Our goal in energy healing is to keep the water (the energy) flowing smoothly throughout the system by clearing the main riverway and the tributaries and dredging any silt that builds up, so to speak.

What is the anatomy of the energy body? The answer to this question depends on the culture and the paradigm of energy healing we're looking at. In Western culture today, the most commonly known paradigms are from traditional Chinese medicine (TCM), which includes the *dan tiens* and *meridians;* the *chakra system* and *aura* from India; and the *matrix* described in several shamanic traditions. These systems have all been written about extensively elsewhere; I will give a brief overview of each, and the references can give you more extensive material.

The Dan Tiens and Meridians

Traditional Chinese medicine is the most complexly mapped system of energy to date. The ancient texts written about TCM go back five thousand years and describe techniques still employed today: herbal medicines, acupuncture, breath, movement, and energy techniques to restore the energy, or *chi (qi)*, balance in the body.

In TCM, there are three primary energy centers, called the dan tiens (figure 1). These are also referred to as separate energy bodies housed within the energy body. The lower dan tien is what regulates or controls the overall energy or vitality of the body. The middle dan tien is responsible for the heart, thymus, throat, and the emotional body; the upper dan tien is responsible for the head and brain and the spiritual body.[11] These energy centers are like wheels of energy within the body. They communicate with each other and with the organs of the body, as well as with the meridians (see figure 2), to influence and affect the function of the body.

In addition, each organ in the body has an energy that communicates with and influences the other organs in the body. For example, the liver can overpower the spleen, or the spleen can affect the heart.

Outside the dan tiens and organs, right under the skin, is the meridian system, a series of linear energy channels throughout the body (figure 2). This meridian system is what acupuncture, acupressure, and many of the body-tapping techniques presented in this book work on.[12]

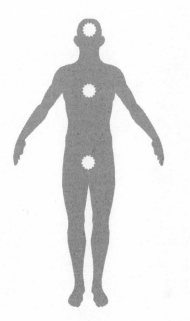 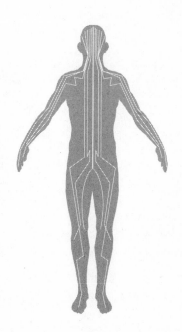

Figure 1: The dan tiens   **Figure 2:** The meridian system

The Chakra System

From India we have the chakra system, described five thousand years ago in a set of texts called the Upanishads. The Upanishads were the first written texts of Indian philosophy that described the origins of health.[13] In the chakra system, the energy body contains seven main wheels or vortices of energy (figure 3), with smaller secondary vortices at each joint. How these main vortices rotate and how they communicate their energy flow with each other controls the health of the body. Each of these chakras has a function and an effect on the body. They affect organ function through a healthy energy flow or lack of flow. For example, at the level of energy, the first chakra is one of the gates, or connection points, to the larger energy field around us (see chapter 2). It connects to and communicates with the larger energy field around us, interpreting the energy from the larger field. To whatever extent this chakra is communicating with the energy field around the body is the extent to which we are *grounded*. (We'll

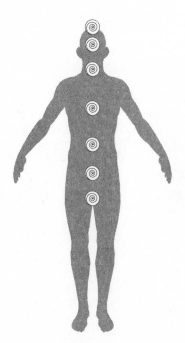

Figure 3: The chakra system

talk more about grounding in chapter 3.) The second chakra takes the energy from the first chakra and transforms it into the body's internal energy, much like the lower dan tien in the Chinese system. In chapter 6, we will discuss the functions of the other chakras and how the chakras work in concert.

The Aura

Connected with the chakra system and also originating from the Hindu tradition, the aura is the aspect of our energy body that radiates out from the physical body and is in constant communication with everything around it (figure 4). When you stand close enough to others, you are within their auric field, and they are within yours. We call this area "personal space," although it extends well beyond what we consider personal space in our culture.

There is an extraordinary amount of information in someone's aura. The Hindu tradition delineates layers of the aura called *kosas*.[14]

Figure 4: The aura

These layers correlate to the chakras and other aspects of an individual, both conscious and unconscious, as well as to the communal layers of the body, which are layers of the energy field that groupings such as couples, families, clans, or cultures actually share. This is a more complex topic than the scope of this book, yet I bring it up here because you may bump into this energy wisdom as you use the material I present in this book.

The Matrix

Oral healing traditions, both in the shamanic traditions and in aboriginal cultures, describe a matrix of energy that is like a grid within the body. This matrix is similar to the Chinese meridian system, yet it is located deeper in the body and is a three-dimensional web of energy made up of very fine filaments of energy (figure 5). The matrix paradigm is becoming more popular in Western culture with the advent of energy techniques that work with it.

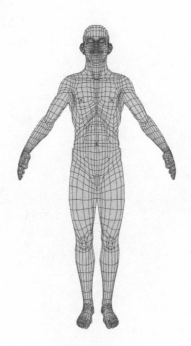

Figure 5: The matrix

I first bumped into the matrix-of-energy system through a psychic surgeon who had trained both in West Africa and in the Yucatán. In the Mexican shamanic, or *nagual,* view, the entire universe is seen as a matrix of filaments of energy.[15] These filaments enter into the body's energy field through an assemblage point and then constellate into the body's energy field. We will explore the assemblage point more in chapter 2. The communication between our body and the energy field around us is constant. Our energy bodies are not separate from the energy flowing in the world around us and energy of other living things in the energy field around us. All the energy healing traditions describe the same thing, though each paradigm defines this connection differently. What I've learned and experienced regarding the matrix in my own study with Yaqui and Mayan healers—and in my explorations of other mystical teachings—matches much of the Egyptian, Hindu, and Tibetan healing philosophies, albeit with different vocabulary.

The Three-Dimensional Energy Body

Different healers perceive, see, and describe the energy body differently, according to how they were trained. As I've studied energy healing over the years, at times I found these differences disconcerting. It was as if I could sense or see only the system I was learning at the time. I approach new modalities as an open-minded skeptic, so at one stage of my journey I began to wonder if I was feeling and sensing in my hands and body because of a brain signal stemming only from my belief from what I was learning at the moment (i.e., my imagination). Later, I experienced another phenomenon: I began to perceive pathways in the body that I knew nothing about. I felt confused as I noticed energy channels that crossed the body and ran up and down in ways that were different than the systems I was familiar with. Each time I noticed these "new" channels, I would check in with one of my teachers, Maria Elena Cairo, and she would confirm that I had stumbled onto something from TCM or another model of health and healing. At that point, I noted how all of these energy anatomies worked together, in the same way the systems of the body—skeletal, muscular, cardiovascular, and so on—work together.

In fact, each of these energy anatomies forms a different layer of the energy body. I believe healers perceive the energy body according to the training they have had; their training teaches them to pitch their attention to the specific anatomy or layer of the energy body their modality works with. Western medical specialists do the same thing, seeing the body through the system they are working with. A cardiologist focuses on the heart and cardiovascular system, but she or he does not look for broken bones. Energy healers have the same partitions; they see the body and treat it from the level of the energy body they were trained in.

How we are taught healing affects both how we see and hold the healing and how we perceive the energy field. This is a key

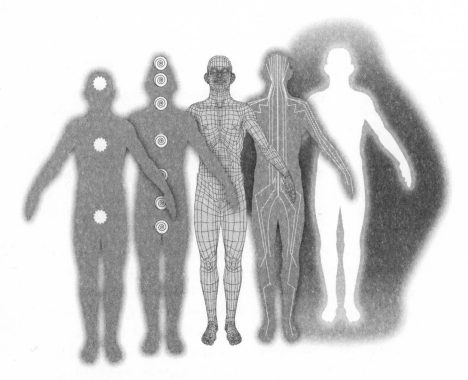

Figure 6: A composite view of the different energy anatomies: At the deepest layer are the dan tiens. Moving outward, there are the chakras, then the matrix, and finally, right under the skin, the meridians. The aura is outside of and around the physical body.

point to keep in mind, as it can be quite confusing for a beginner to understand why different energy healers may have such different and varied explanations and therapies for the same dynamic in one individual.

In this composite view of the different energy anatomies, at the deepest layer are the dan tiens. As we move toward the skin, we have the chakras, then the matrix, and finally, right under the skin, the meridians. The aura extends out beyond the body—between twenty and thirty feet or beyond, depending on which layer of the aura we are working with. Figure 6 shows how I see the composite energy body and the different anatomies working together. I am sure these maps are an unrefined description of what is happening, yet they help structure the way we interact with the energy body.

ILLNESS, TRAUMA, AND THE ENERGY BODY

Ordinarily, illness develops when there is a problem in the energy body. In the natural history of a disease, the energy body first becomes blocked or unbalanced. Over time, disease develops, and, finally, symptoms appear in the physical body. Major diseases typically appear years after a disruption in the natural flow of energy has begun, depending on the location and severity of the block or imbalance (see figure 7).

I'll use the example of a case I saw many years ago in my office to clarify this concept of the natural history of disease. A woman came to see me with chronically itchy legs. Her symptoms were so uncomfortable that she had scabbing all over her lower limbs from scratching so much. In her case, first there was an energy block in the legs and hips, so the energy flow was not moving through her legs properly. Next, she had pathology develop (inflammation in the lower limbs), then symptoms of intense itching. She went to a dermatologist, who prescribed steroids. This is usually an effective treatment for this type of neurodermatitis, yet the steroids did not work.

A month or so later, she came into my office, and I prescribed a technique called Toe Tapping (see chapter 3) for the underlying energy cause. Within a month, she was symptom free, and her legs

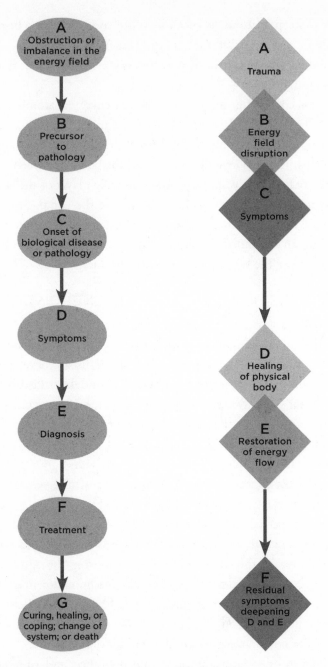

Figure 7: The natural progression of illness in the energy body and physical body

Figure 8: The natural progression of trauma in the energy body and physical body

had healed. (Had I seen her before the dermatologist, I would have prescribed both the steroids and the Toe Tapping, as I use all the modalities that can work with a diagnosis, not only energy healing techniques.) A few years later she returned to my office, as the itching had begun again. I encouraged her to start the Toe Tapping again to move the stagnant energy in her legs, and her symptoms resolved immediately.

The key point is that the energy imbalance occurs first, before any symptoms or pathology in most cases of illness and disease. Once the pathology is present, using conventional medicine with all other effective modalities is best, and working with the energy body during the entire process will facilitate healing more quickly.

While disease takes time to develop, pain (a symptom that comes from blocked energy) can occur right away. In the case of trauma, the energy field is disrupted at the same time as the physical body. After the initial disruption, the symptom, pain, occurs. Then the healing occurs at the level of the energy body simultaneously or before it occurs in the physical body. Residual symptoms occur usually because of a residual energy obstruction or an inadequate physical healing (see figure 8).

The healing of the physical body and energy body are not separate; working with the energy flow can speed physical healing and help with restoration of normal physical functioning. We can see this with the case of a broken bone. The energy field is disrupted at the same time as the bone breaks. As the bone mends, the flow of energy also comes back into alignment as much as possible. Residual symptoms, such as aching after increased activity or with weather changes, can be addressed at the level of the energy body. Using energy exercises to restore energy flow can alleviate the long-term residual symptoms, if there are any, after the bone has healed.

Weaknesses in the immune system leading to infection are also dependent on the energy flow in the body. This is one reason why not everyone in a household may catch the current cold going around, or why some people can fight off penetrating organisms while others become ill. In fact, the body may work around an infection, such as with an abscess. An abscess is the body's way of trying to return to homeostasis, even though bacteria or organisms have intruded and taken hold. The body will wall off the infection, and the energy flow will move around the abscess.

WHAT IS HEALING?

The energy body is the underlying flow of energy that assists and supports the body's normal functioning. While we talk about the energy body and the flow of energy as two different things, they are, in fact, one entity. The energy body is a body of energy in constant flow and movement. We can assist the health of the energy body and the flow of energy by opening energy channels and allowing sluggish or stagnant energy to flow in its natural patterns. Illness, symptoms, and energy blocks all occur in an effort to bring an energy pattern back to its natural flow. It is important to stress that healing is the restoration of the underlying flow in the body. Healing is the unwinding of energy blocks. Healing is redemption of a wound that has been inflicted or an illness that has appeared. Healing is the movement of the energy body back toward wholeness, back toward its original pattern, albeit with imperfection or scars and often with change.

This healing process requires a remarkable symphony of factors. With illness, the illness itself can be part of a healing response. The energetically weak area becomes involved in illness, and through the healing of the problem, the energy flow and the physical body return to homeostasis and balance. The illness is the resolution of the conflict at the level of energy. From this perspective, illness is the beginning of healing at the level of the energy body. The body is moving toward healing, so the illness constellates to make up for the chronic or acute energy problem in the body. The idea that illness is serving the healing process is a radically different way of viewing illness, and it will allow for a deep appreciation of the wisdom of the body. The body is clever, amazing, and incredible.

The physical site of a disease, pain, or other problem does not always correspond exactly with the blocked spot in the energy body.

With leg problems, for instance, the pain or the physical issue might be at the foot or the knee, but the energy block is often at the hip (figure 9).

In the chakra anatomy system, the disease often manifests in an area of the physical body that is one or two chakras away from the energy block. When I was experiencing morning sickness with my first pregnancy, an energy healer worked weekly at my solar plexus chakra, the chakra responsible for the stomach, but the nausea didn't go away. In fact, it would get worse, and I would gag on the table. Then one week, she worked deeply at my high heart, in my upper chest, between my fourth and fifth chakras, and we both felt the energy pop and move. It was so dramatic that we both said, "Oh!" aloud at the same time. The intense nausea I'd had was gone from that moment on. The block had been in my chest, but the symptoms

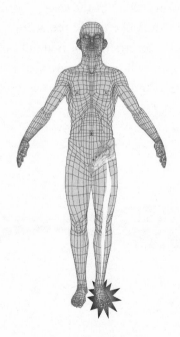

Figure 9: The physical site of a disease, pain, or other problem does not always match the blocked spot in the energy body. For instance, pain in the knee or foot often stems from an energy block at the hip.

had been both above and below the block, in my gagging throat and in my upset stomach. (I learned later that the high heart is a place where we work with and store fear; think of how you catch your breath when you are afraid, or how asthma attacks often include anxiety. Perhaps the healer was able to open the blocked flow because I had finally aligned with the huge shift that was coming with having my first child and, thus, I was ready to release my fear about the change.) In chapter 10, we'll explore in more detail the connection between illness and injuries in the physical body and blocks in the energy body.

WHAT CAUSES ENERGY BLOCKS OR IMBALANCES, AND HOW CAN THEY BE CLEARED?

When energy healers talk about a block or an imbalance, we normally mean a place in the energy body where the flow of energy is sluggish or not moving along at the pace it would in a healthy or unblocked energy body. I like to use the analogy of plumbing in a house. If a pipe has a constriction or buildup inside it, the flow of water through the pipe will not be as brisk as in an unblocked pipe (figure 10). Further, pressure will build up behind the constriction in

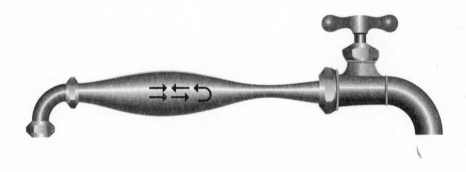

Figure 10: A block in the energy body is like a block in a water pipe. Constriction or buildup in the pipe (the energy body) restricts the flow of water (energy), causing a backup or overflow behind the block and a paucity in front of it.

the pipe, making the pipe weaker and perhaps causing it to spring a leak. Energy pathways also get congested, and they overflow. We experience this overflow often as heat and inflammation in the physical body. In addition, the block will result in a lower flow of energy farther along the path, because the energy is building up at the block instead of moving through at an unobstructed pace. If we look back at the block of energy in the hip, not only can there be pain in the hip, knee, or ankle, there will also be less energy flowing into the lower abdomen area. This person would likely feel more tired, as his or her core energy would be diminished. Instead of receiving energy through the right and the left hip, he or she would receive only a strong flow up the unaffected leg.

There is a myriad of things that can cause a block or imbalance in the energy flow of the body, and they're the same things that are seen to cause disease and illness in conventional medicine. They include external insults, like toxins or bacteria; genetic or hereditary causes; and physical or emotional trauma.

Transferring energy, which we can practice with touch, breath, and sound, is actually adding energy into an area. We can add more energy through a low-flow or blocked area, and over time the channel will open. Removing blocks in the energy body means breaking up blocks and tangles in the matrix, chakras, or dan tiens to help the energy move through them naturally in order to align the energy body as a whole. We can use movement and other techniques to allow the body's own energy to do both—to remove blocks and add energy—at the same time. This allows energy to move between parts of the body, from overflow or stagnant areas to low-flow areas. Except in the case of pain, the difference between transferring energy, moving energy, and opening blocks becomes a bit of an extraneous point, as these three realities are working in a harmonious symphony. The key is to keep the entire energy body clear and open so the energy flowing promotes health and healing.

Pain is the result of blocked energy, and chronic pain indicates blocks that have been around for some time. When there is an energy block, an energy healing technique adds energy to the system, increasing energy flow to the area where there is decreased flow, which results in more energy at the site of the block. Adding energy into an energy system with multiple energy blocks can cause an increase in pain if you do not move slowly and, at the same time, seek to open the flow in blocked areas.

In some ways, energy healing is more about preventing disease and illness than healing them, because working with the energy body allows us to notice and resolve areas of difficulty before disease or illness shows up in the physical body. Once a disease is present in the physical body, conventional treatment is often required, although energy healing techniques are usually wonderful adjuncts to conventional treatment.

When I first started using energy healing techniques, a friend asked me to work on her. While she lay on the floor, I scanned her aura. I noticed that something was different in the level of the energy body at her lower abdomen. Compared to the energy of the rest of her body, there was a different consistency in her aura in that area. I remember telling her it felt like I was running my hand over gravel.

A few months later, she called me from the hospital. She had gone to the emergency room with pain in her lower left abdomen. A CT scan found a very large tumor, the size of a grapefruit, in her ovary—"right where you noticed that day," she told me. As my friend had a larger build, she had not been able to feel a bump or fullness in her abdomen up to that point. After her surgery to remove the tumor, as she was recovering in the hospital, I visited her and did more energy healing work on her every day. She later told me that she had recovered and was able to leave the hospital faster than her medical team had expected. They were surprised by how soon they could let her go home. Not only did the energy field inform me where her problem was initially, but the energy healing in the hospital also helped with her recovery—with clearing the anesthetic used in the surgery, with wound healing, and with getting her up and around.[16]

HOW CAN WE MOVE ENERGY
THROUGH THE ENERGY BODY?

Energy can be moved in the energy body through movement, touch, sound and vibration, the breath, electricity or current, light, and magnets. Even wind, rain, or sunlight can move energy in our bodies, the same way they move energy in our environment. Try this: stand in a strong wind and notice how you feel afterwards—more clear and more energized. You may do the same with rain or sun. Even standing next to a tree may begin to move energy in your body. Pets are the best example of how natural forces can affect our energy. It is well documented that pets have a healing effect on us; it is the effect of their energy field, and the power of energy transfer through touch, that results in this healing shift.

In this book, we will explore movement, hands-on healing, sound, and breath as means of moving energy. Moving the physical body promotes energy flow throughout the energy body, and it enhances energy flow throughout the entire energy body, not just one area. Rigorous exercise is a means of moving energy, but even small movements can have a profound impact as the area being moved impacts the flow in the rest of the body. Many of the energy healing techniques I use and include in this book make use of movement.

While our entire body can be used to move energy, our hands are very sensitive and have more nerve endings than most other parts of the body. Our hands also run a small amount of measureable current and can transfer energy into the body with ease.[17] Touch is the most common and instinctual way we transfer energy. It works on our own bodies and on the bodies of others we touch. We'll explore Sacred Touch, a healing form of touch specifically designed to move energy within the body. We will also focus our attention on tapping techniques that move energy through mechanical vibration and small movements. I also love using a handheld massager, which moves energy very quickly and breaks up energy blocks the same way it breaks up tension or a knot in a muscle.

Sound moves energy through sound waves and mechanical vibration. Sound also entrains the nervous system and brain-wave functions of the body—meaning that sound goes into and directly affects these parts of the body. Rattles, for example, are used in many healing traditions. Both the sound and the vibration they produce rapidly and effectively break up stagnant energy.

Finally, focused breath can move energy within the energy body in a profound way, as it is using both attention and awareness. We will explore multiple breathing techniques in chapter 5. Several of the techniques described in this book use specific breathing patterns to move energy in particular ways.

THE BENEFITS OF ENERGY HEALING

Energy healing means keeping the energy body as clear as possible and the energy flowing through it in a healthy way. A healthy body adapts—this is the body's ability to move energy naturally in response to an influx of energy or a block that occurs due to trauma or illness. A healthy energy body will promote health, increase your vitality, and also help prevent disease and illness from developing. If you are already healthy, then using energy healing techniques to restore and maintain energetic balance will enable you to see what is occurring in your energy body as you become more aware of the energy flow. If you have had surgery or are ill or injured, working with your energy body can help you speed up healing in your physical body. If you are experiencing pain or a chronic illness, you will notice that using energy healing on yourself over time will begin to move blocks in your body and begin your journey back to energy balance and adaptation.

Here is the way I see health and healing happening in the energy healing paradigm: first we need to open the body and ground it, then we can clear it of old and recent blocks, and finally we can go in and do specific repair work. This is the model that the practices in this book are based on.

Many energy healing techniques act as adaptogens with the body. The concept of an adaptogen is not commonly held in our culture, yet it is well described and used in botanical medicine and traditional Chinese medicine. An adaptogen is a therapy, herb, or intervention that brings the body back to homeostasis—back into balance from whatever extreme it has moved to. For example, if the body has moved into the extreme of low blood pressure, an adaptogen would increase blood pressure, yet the same adaptogen would decrease blood pressure in someone with blood pressure that is too high. The same herb or therapy, used on both low and high blood pressure, would result in a person having a more normal or healthy blood pressure. In energy healing, the same technique can often increase energy in a part of the body where energy is low and decrease it in another area where energy is too high.

One of the most important ways energy healing enhances our health is by decreasing anxiety. We know that the relaxation benefits of energy healing have an impact on health. In the 1970s, Dr. Herbert Benson's work demonstrated that relaxation improves blood pressure and heart rate and enhances immune-system function, gastrointestinal peristalsis, kidney function, and brain-wave activity.[18] Energy healing modalities are thought to function through relaxation or in a fashion similar to relaxation, shifting autonomic-nervous-system function to improve health and reduce inflammation. It is now becoming apparent in conventional medicine that most or all disease starts as inflammation, and the autonomic nervous system affects the overall inflammation in the body. This means that tending to inflammation and to the nervous system, as energy healing techniques do, may be an important way to keep the body healing itself and to prevent disease.

The depth of the effect of energy modalities may also explain why energy balance is so important in many paradigms of health and healing, yet so difficult to research. It may be involved in the earliest stages of illness and disease and too early to detect with our outcomes-based research.

THE BODY MOVES TOWARD SELF-HEALING

As explained earlier, healing can be defined as our body moving back toward its original pattern of wholeness. The body is constantly bringing itself back to homeostasis (balance and wholeness) by healing, detoxifying, and adapting. The symptom or illness is often not a problem, but the body's resolution to the conflict of excess energy.

Creating symptoms, illnesses, and pain are how the body manages non-wholeness.

We often take it for granted that the body moves naturally toward self-healing. Think of any cut or blister you have had. It naturally healed over the period of a few days, and the process involved a remarkable symphony of factors. A natural flow toward healing also occurs within the energy body; in fact, the energy body's natural flow toward healing assists with the physical body's normal functioning. We help both the energy body and our physical body to heal by opening energy channels and allowing sluggish or stagnant energy to flow in its natural patterns.

I began to notice how the body moves back to homeostasis after I began to delve deeply into energy healing work. As I practiced energy healing techniques regularly, I became balanced and healthy. The long-term energy blocks that had caused my chronic pain disappeared, and my body would respond and react energetically as it was meant to, healing itself quickly and efficiently. I still pulled muscles or injured myself or became ill at times, yet if I worked with the energy body, healing could move along very quickly—and it still does.

I first saw that the energy healing practices were really working when I pulled a muscle slightly one day in the course of running around after my two toddlers. I had a sore neck and shoulder, like I was beginning to get a crick in my neck. I could still turn my head, yet there was a noticeable sensation in my neck and shoulder. That evening, when I crawled into bed, I lay on my back and placed my hands over my thighs to balance the flow in my energy body. Then I relaxed, dropped my hands to my side, and began to drift off to sleep. When I was almost asleep, I heard a slight buzz in my right ear, and my right arm began to shake and lift off the bed, almost as if it were having a spasm. My arm twitched up, off the bed, and back down. After about ten seconds, both the movement and the buzzing stopped, and I noticed my neck and shoulder were no longer sore or tight. The blocked energy had discharged itself and cleared the path; the muscle relaxed. The energy body's natural self-healing mechanism was doing its job as I was drifting off to sleep.

THE BODY AS TEACHER

My eldest daughter taught me an incredible lesson in energy when she was an infant. Just after she was born, on the second or third day she was home with me, we were lying side by side on the couch, and I was watching her falling asleep. She closed her eyes and raised her arms, her thumbs and forefingers touching in what looked like a traditional yoga *mudra,* or hand position. Her breath quickened, her hands stayed up, and she began to breathe in a pattern that in yoga is referred to as "the breath of fire," a way of breathing that moves energy with repeated, rapid exhalations. She breathed this way for a minute or so, then fell asleep. While she slept, her hands stayed up in the air for more than thirty minutes.

The body is an energy machine, and it naturally puts movement and positions together with the breath for relaxation, sleep, and healing. My daughter's little body was just doing what came naturally to it. Her arm movement, hand position, and way of breathing mirrored yoga techniques because yoga techniques are designed to flow from the natural movements of the body.

My dear friend Keith experienced a dramatic story of this innate healing wisdom in the body spontaneously presenting itself. Keith had a serious case of temporomandibular joint (TMJ) syndrome, otherwise called "lockjaw." His jaw muscles became tight and could not move. Unable to open his jaw or chew functionally, he began to lose weight. It was time to try everything possible. Having had a lot of spiritual and meditation training, Keith one day lay flat on a couch and relaxed. He went into a deep state of relaxation and asked his body how it could heal itself. He continued to relax as deeply as he could. After a bit of time, Keith's right arm came off the couch, moved across his body, and pulled his body onto the floor. He chose not to stop this process, but become a witness to it. He found himself rolling around the floor of his living room for three hours. He moved and moved and moved some more, his body taking on unusual postures as it wiggled and rolled around. When he woke up the next morning, he went into the living room and allowed this spontaneous movement to take over again. It became his daily practice, for hours a day.

Within a month, his jaw was healed, fine, and mobile; he could eat, sing, and chew.

Keith knew he was onto something different, so he continued his daily movement practice. After a period of time, he noticed that his body was drawn into the same poses over and over. He did some research and found that these poses were ancient yoga poses. Keith believes he underwent a spontaneous unwinding experience or a spontaneous *pranotthanic* experience. The energy in his body began to take over and lead him into a spontaneous healing experience through movement and breath work that brought him into a full energy alignment and energy balance. All of the energy stagnations that occurred through his lifetime cleared over a period of months.

Keith's story and my experience with my infant daughter illustrate how the body is both a teacher and a map; we are its students, and we are on its journey. Most energy healing techniques—whether they involve movement, breathing, or other means of shifting energy—originated in the body itself. Someone sat and dropped into body awareness or, like Keith, was presented with a map, and a technique was born. I do not think it is possible to invent an energy healing technique that does not actually come from the body; instead, we can only harvest new techniques from the body. No one can own the wisdom of the body, because the body will reveal its wisdom to anyone diligent enough to seek it.

HEALING AT THE PACE OF THE ENERGY BODY

Keith's healing was a result of devoting time to healing activities. He was patient and spent hours a day on unwinding, trusting his body to heal itself. I figure he did this unwinding for sixty hours before his jaw unlocked and healed back into flexibility. In our "take a pill," instant-fix culture, his story is inspiring.

Healing can take years, or it can happen in an instant. Normally, it takes time. When a bone breaks, it knits itself back together when set in the proper position and given time. Even after the bone is whole again, the healing process continues as the limb recovers its strength and is restored to full function. If we look back several years later, we might see that the bone took six weeks to mend, then it took another few months for the limb's full function to return, and then it perhaps took years before the site of the break no longer gave pain signals on rainy days. This is the natural pace of healing with the physical body.

Time is also the key to healing with the energy body. Normally, we must use an energy-moving exercise daily over three or four months, not just once, before we see and feel an effect. Once we begin to work with the energy body, a symptom, illness, or pain often changes. Total healing may not result immediately, yet symptoms change, illnesses lessen their impact on our lives, and pain decreases. The body may not be back to wholeness, yet some healing has occurred. Healing happens in stages. Sometimes the shifts in healing happen so slowly that we do not notice them until we look back and see that we are in much better shape now than a year ago. In another year, our symptoms, illnesses, or pain may slip away altogether.

ENERGY HEALING AND CHRONIC PAIN

Chronic pain and chronic-pain syndromes, such as fibromyalgia, require special care with energy healing. If you're using energy healing because you have chronic pain, you will need to move slowly into the techniques in this book. Adding too much energy into your energy system can make you feel great at first, but if you continue adding too much too quickly, you may experience increased pain before the pain goes away completely. If you have a chronic-pain syndrome, shorten the movement exercises for the first week or so and then move up to the full exercises over the first month.

As I mentioned in the introduction, I had a chronic-pain syndrome on and off for thirty years. I was born with an abnormality in my left kidney called a dual collecting system. Basically, I had a normal kidney on the right side, but two kidneys fused together on the left side, with two ureters that drained into my bladder. One of the ureters was set into my bladder in a way that it did not function normally, so I had urinary reflux from my bladder into my kidney whenever my bladder was full or when I lay flat. The result was chronic bladder and kidney infections from ages of four to thirty-four, along with chronic pelvic and back pain.

Normally this problem would have been repaired in childhood, but for various reasons, I did not have this condition fully diagnosed and repaired surgically until I was an adult. After I had the extra part of my kidney and the extra ureter removed, the pain continued, although there was no longer any medical reason for it. I understood that the pain pathways in my pelvis area were being activated and were firing regardless of the lack of infections. I began to deeply explore the concept of the energy body being blocked. I explored energy healing techniques and saw energy healers to try to resolve the chronic pain.

Initially, after every healing session I received, the pain flared up for two or three hours. I would lie on a healer's table and become totally relaxed; she would run energy through my body with her hands, and then I would go home and experience a flare-up. This became a reproducible pattern for the first few hours after energy work, ceremony work, or even strenuous exercise. Any influx of energy would cause pain for a few hours, and then the pain would resolve without any antibiotics or medicine.

Because I understood what was happening at the level of the energy body, I continued to receive energy sessions and to use energy healing techniques to open the channels of energy. Change happened slowly, over time; discomfort after an energy influx would lessen until it finally resolved. The initial improvement happened quickly, over about nine months, but the total resolution took four years.

I tell this story for those of you with chronic pain. Full healing takes time, and you must move consistently and slowly for the energy blocks to clear. I have seen occasional spontaneous healings, yet for most chronic pain, healing takes time.

People with chronic pain often experience the pattern I did. They have an energy session and feel great for a day or two afterward, and then they have a terrible flare-up of the pain (see figure 11). The problem with chronic pain is that we end up in a syndrome with it; the mind tends to think the last thing that helped the pain is the "cure" and the last event that triggered a flare-up of the pain is the "cause." Every flare-up of the pain feels as if the problem has gone back to ground zero or worse, when actually the pain pattern is improving. We see the situation this way because suffering chronic pain causes a form of quiet desperation that cannot see the entire history and pattern of the pain clearly. In this case, we have to look at symptoms over time to assess progress. It is best to partner with a practitioner who can help us sort out the syndrome and continue to give us encouragement.

The other problem with chronic pain is that when the pain is gone, we want to get on with normal life, so activities that are good for preventing and treating the pain fall by the wayside on the good days, but then can be too painful to do on the bad days. I sympathize fully with how difficult this balance can be. Perhaps those who have not experienced chronic pain cannot really relate to the cycle of hope and despair that goes along with pain.

I suggest you practice the techniques in this book for at least nine months. This may seem like a long time, yet if you look at how long you have had the pain, it makes sense to give energy-moving techniques a good long trial.

Finally, you have to keep doing the practices after the pain resolves, or it may return. Time after time I have clients who, after a complete

Figure 11: With chronic pain, energy healing can lead to flare-ups in the short term, but gradual improvement over the long term.

resolution of their symptoms, return when the symptoms come back again. Each time I ask, "Are you still doing the techniques daily?" Each time they say, "Oh, no, I stopped when the pain/chronic infection/headaches went away." I advise them to go back to the practices, and when they do, the symptoms resolve again. It is human nature to stop doing the thing that helped, once we are better. I encourage clients to continue the practices for the rest of their lives, especially if they have had a chronic-pain syndrome that lasted for years.

CHAPTER 2

Connecting into the Unified Energy Field and the Shamanic Field

> *If I could control the channels of my breath*
> *If I could perform precise surgery on myself*
> *I could create the substance that awareness is*
>
> —Lalla, *Naked Song*

Our energy is not ours; it is part of a larger energy field. How we are connected to that larger field of energy, often called the *unified energy field,* affects both our vitality and our ability to sense and be aware of energy. This unified energy field encompasses not only our individual energy fields, but also the energy fields of everything that exists in the universe. This includes electromagnetic fields of celestial bodies such as the moon and the sun—both of which strongly influence our individual fields—as well as the energy field of the earth. Because we reside on the earth, the earth's electromagnetic field is the strongest planetary field we humans are in contact with.

The human body, I have come to realize, is not separate from the physical world around it. The body (both the physical and energy body) is actually part of the living energy field of the earth; the earth is the larger body we are all involved with and part of, which is why working with the earth's energy field is a key part of the energy-healing practices I use. And the best paradigm I've found for using the earth's field for energy healing is the paradigm of shamanism.

SHAMANISM AND THE SHAMANIC FIELD

Shamanism is difficult to define. The clearest definition of a shaman I have found comes from Dr. Michael Harner, founder of the Foundation for Shamanic Studies: "The word 'shaman' in the original Tungus language refers to a person who makes journeys to nonordinary reality in an altered state of consciousness. Adopting the term in the West was useful because people didn't know what it meant. Terms like 'wizard,' 'witch,' 'sorcerer,' and 'witch doctor' have their own connotations, ambiguities, and preconceptions associated with them. Although the term is from Siberia, the practice of shamanism existed on all inhabited continents."[1]

A shaman, to me, is one who works with the energy fields of the human body, nature, and the earth. Shamans are in relationship with the entire unified field of energy, and primarily the earth's energy field. Shamans read, respond to, and act in accordance with the earth's energy, as well as with the energies of the weather, animals, the human body, and all other creatures. They see the energy of all these things as one fluent flow.

Michael Harner writes about the same set of realities and realizations I've encountered in my journeys and learning. He says, "What's really important about shamanism is that there is another reality that you can personally discover . . . [W]e are not alone."[2] He also says, "Much shamanic work . . . is done in darkness for a very simple reason. The shaman wishes to cut out the stimuli of ordinary reality—light, sound, and so on—and move into unseen reality. The shaman learns to look in the body with 'x-ray vision' and see the illness and its location, and then to extract that illness."[3] To me, what shamans are seeing with this "x-ray vision" is the *shamanic field*, the energy field that is both within the body and within the natural world. The shamanic field is the part of the greater unified energy field that we access through both our physical body and our energy body. Shamans read reality at the level of energy; this requires that shamans read energy in the natural world and in the body. Whether someone sees it, senses it, feels it, or has another way of interacting with the energy, it is reading reality and working with reality at the level of energy that facilitates this connection with nature. The reverse is true as well; it is this connection with the natural world at the level of energy that allows shamans to read reality at the level of energy.

This shamanic view is different from that of indigenous priests and priestesses and other healers who are in touch with what might be called the upper aspects of the unified energy field. While shamans connect with the lower aspects of the unified energy field—the earth and its energy field, temporality, the natural world, all things physical—others connect with the upper aspects, such as spiritual beings, nonphysical dimensions of the universe, and the energy fields of celestial bodies. These priestly healers typically connect "up to the heavens" instead of connecting "down to" the earth and the natural world. Their work can be profound, yet they are not reading the shamanic field or the energy of the natural world per se. Mayan priests, for example, were connected to the sun, stars, and heavens and were greatly served by that connection. By staying connected to "the above," they could read much of the pattern of things to come. In fact, they built pyramids in their communities to facilitate this connection with the celestial bodies, and they were able to bring through or receive tremendous amounts of information through their connections.

Shamans can move energy and connect to the larger energy field around them in profound ways. While we are not all shamans, we can all connect to the shamanic field. Once we learn to connect to it, we can also learn to read it and harvest our own wisdom from it. Connecting to and reading this field of energy takes trial and error—and practice.

Consciousness is held within the unified field of energy. In fact, awareness and consciousness are the substance of the energy field, which could also be called the *unified field of awareness*. This perspective goes against many current modalities that describe "getting conscious" or "being conscious." As humans, we have appropriated consciousness for ourselves. But actually, it is the energy field that holds the awareness or consciousness, and that means the amount of consciousness or awareness available to each of us in any moment depends on how strongly we are connected to the shamanic field. Since this book's material is pitched to connecting with the body, we will stay with the term *shamanic field*. We can use this term and the *unified field of awareness* interchangeably; the only difference between the two is how we connect to the larger energy field.

It is how we connect to the shamanic field through our own energy body that determines what information we have access to. The Yaqui model of the *assemblage point* describes this idea best. In the Yaqui tradition, the assemblage point is where the energy of the shamanic field comes into the body and is translated into our personal reality. "The impact of the energy fields going through the assemblage point was transformed into sensory data; data which were then interpreted into the cognition of the world of everyday life," wrote Carlos Castaneda in his book *The Teachings of Don Juan*.[4] When the assemblage point "was at a new position, a different bundle of energy fields went through it, forcing the assemblage point to turn those energy fields into sensory data and interpret them, giving as a result a veritable new world to perceive," he adds.[5]

How we connect to this larger field determines how we see and access healing, knowledge, and awareness or consciousness. And it is how we are connected and how we are aware of this connection that allows us to read reality at the level of energy. The Yaqui model speaks of the matrix of energy and the assemblage point, yet we can use the model of the chakras and find a connection to the shamanic field through each separate chakra; we will do this in chapter 6. We can also use the TCM model of the dan tiens, which we will also explore in chapter 6. The key is that when we connect to this shamanic field of energy in one way, the reality we see at the level of energy looks one way. If we can connect to the shamanic field through multiple assemblage points, chakras, or dan tiens, then we have access to more awareness, vitality, and information. There is increased inner resource and stimulation available when we can hold more than one state of consciousness, more than one assemblage point, or more than one connection point to the larger conscious field.

I want to stress that the unified field is a magnetic field of energy moving toward healing, life, and death in a way that follows laws of energy and awareness. Our individual energy fields are connected to this shamanic field all the time, but we have muted our senses to block most of this information. You can open the aperture of your awareness to connect more deeply and in multiple ways at once. Connect primarily through the lower body energy centers, and we're connected to the natural world and what I am calling the shamanic field. Connect through the upper chakras or centers, and we are in another field, often called universal energy. It is all the unified field of energy. I use *shamanic field* here to differentiate and stress the connection to the larger energy field through the lower body, or through the lower body in conjunction with the heart and upper chakras, if one is able to hold more than two states or points of awareness.

I learned firsthand just how powerful the unified energy field is through an experience I had in the winter of 2002. I was in Dziuche, a small town in Quintana Roo, Mexico, on a healing journey with a group led by one of my teachers, Maria Elena Cairo. We were visiting a psychic surgeon named Don Jorge Gomez. I want to give you a detailed picture of Don Jorge so you may take this journey with me as I went to see this amazing healer. I also want to convey to you what is possible when one reads reality at the level of energy.

Don Jorge had a life story that exemplifies the traumatic childhood and wounding that are common for extraordinary healers. The dance of the difficult, chaotic childhood often gives someone the ability to read reality in a different way, hence moving the person toward personal healing (sometimes desperately needed) and energy work. This is important: the wounding you received in your life is what allows you access to self-healing work at a deep level. It is also what pushes you toward self-healing.

Don Jorge was half African and half Mayan. His Mayan mother had become pregnant by an African man, who had returned to Africa when Jorge was born. When Jorge was young, his mother sold Jorge to an American woman who lived in Los Angeles. He loved his adoptive mother and was devastated when she died; he was nine. His African father was contacted, and within a week after his adoptive mother's death, Jorge was in Africa.

His biological father took Jorge to the bush and dropped him off with a medicine man for training. He spent years in the bush, learning indigenous healing techniques. Later, Jorge went to a school in Kenya that trained psychic surgeons. Psychic surgery is a high-velocity energy-movement process. There are multiple forms of this process in the world. In Asia, psychic surgeons use their hands to penetrate the energy body. The form of psychic surgery Jorge learned involved using scissors to work in both the aura and the parts of the energy body that are within the physical body.

In Dziuche, the other group members and I would go very early in the mornings to Don Jorge's clinic for his diagnostic sessions. We lined up and waited for our ten seconds in front of him, each of us holding an unfertilized egg in our left hand. We would go in, one by one, and sit in front of his desk. He would take the egg, crack it into a glass of water, and read it with a magnifying glass. He was an extraordinary diagnostician. He would diagnose exactly what was affecting us in the moment, as well as all the major illnesses each of us had had in our lives. Often when I was sitting in front of him, he would comment on the deeper desire for my trip, such as "learning to move past fear" or "stronger energy running through my hands." He could read the reality of my body and soul in an unveiled, uncanny way. He was looking into my body and soul, reading my health and development on multiple levels.

After the morning diagnostic session, we would line up and wait for the rounds of surgeries to be called. When it was our turn, each of us would hurriedly climb on a clinic table, where an attendant would uncover the part of our body Don Jorge would be working on. He came to the table, scissors in hand, splashed us with antibacterial solution, and made his cuts at a speed that was too fast to see. When I watched him work on me, his hands moved so quickly that it was hard to see what was happening; however, I could feel sensations inside my body as well as on my skin. When I had the chance to peek at what he was doing, it appeared that the scissors blades disappeared into my body, as if they were cutting inside the physical body. When he was finished with the surgery, which took five to ten seconds, there were small incisions that looked like scratches already healing on my skin. The amount of energy moved was enormous, and a few times I saw heavy bruising under my skin, even though it didn't feel like much had happened.

The healings I experienced and witnessed were remarkable. I went one time with a chronic, spasmodic cough that had been present for a week. One surgery to my lungs, and the cough was completely gone. Heartburn and gallbladder pain also resolved with one surgery and never returned. The most remarkable story from our group was that of a woman with astigmatism and visual problems, for which she wore bifocals. After one surgery to her eyes, she no longer needed to wear glasses. Other stories from our group and from Don Jorge's community documented cancers and other serious illnesses resolved with one surgery or a series of surgeries.

Even more profound than the healings from the surgeries was the experience I had of being in the town of Dziuche—an experience that was my initiation into the unified field of awareness. Don Jorge would perform three or four rounds of psychic surgery each day. Between rounds, exhausted from the flow of energy that had been working through him, he would return to his house in the village for a break. All of the workers at his clinic would return to their homes as well. About five minutes before he left his house to return to the clinic, all the workers would begin walking back. There was no regular timing to these breaks, and there was no external or audible communication between the clinic workers and Don Jorge. This form of nonverbal communication was happening in Dziuche all day long.

I'd made several trips to the village and to Don Jorge's clinic over the years, but on that trip in late 2002, I began to catch the "wave" that the clinic workers were catching. I could feel a vibrational message going out, and I would be moved to stand and get ready to go back to the clinic as the clinic workers did. And then, sure enough, here would come Don Jorge. We were all receiving energetic messages from him just because we'd been spending time in his energetic field. Initially I thought it was just the strength of Don Jorge's personal field that moved us all. However, I have since come to know that he was following the larger field of awareness, as we all were. It was the field of energy that dictated the entire movement, including his healing work. We were all, including Don Jorge, reading what was about to happen and responding to it.

I had a similar experience when I worked on a First Nations reserve in northern Canada. The doctors there talked about the "moccasin telegraph." After a family member had come into the hospital, the entire family would show up, without any of us at the hospital having told them that their family member was there. There were no cell phones on the reserve, and when I asked the family who had called them, they looked perplexed. This is what happens when two opposing realities collide: my question made no sense to them, just as their ability to simply show up made no sense to me. A good analogy would be if someone asked you why you brought an umbrella to work when it had been raining as you left your house. "What kind of a question is that?" you'd probably think. Perhaps then you would realize that because the other person had not been outside or looked out a window since the day before, he or she had no connection to what was happening in the natural world. Those connected into the unified field of energy at the level of nature—those connected to the shamanic field—are in touch with information that is unavailable to those who are not. We will discuss this connection at the level of nature later in this book.

EFFECTS OF CONNECTING TO
THE SHAMANIC FIELD

One morning on another of my trips to Dziuche, I awoke in the hotel with a buzzing sensation between my legs, in my perineal and sacral area. It felt as if a bee were trapped inside my body. I paid close attention. What was this?

Two friends I was with noticed the vibration, too.

"Do you feel that?" one asked the other. "The vibration?"

"Yes."

I was stunned, knowing that what they were feeling was coming from inside me. Some connection had opened in my body. It was like an inner motor. I knew it was a connection through to the unified field of energy through the root chakra—connection at the level of the shamanic field.

After this experience, my sensitivity to the entire unified field of energy heightened dramatically; it was as if I were living with all my faculties for the first time. I was amazed. I had somehow been reconnected with the web of energy that the entire world was feeding on, living on—or maybe not reconnected, but connected a new, different way. For example, I began to notice birds flying by—notice them not with my eyes or ears, but with my energy body. With my eyes closed, I would feel a movement above me and then notice the bird. I played with this phenomenon: closing my eyes, noticing a sensation in my energy field, and then opening my eyes to see what I was noticing in much the same way I would check lab tests to clarify what I was perceiving after I'd scanned someone's energy field. People walking far away caused energy disturbances I felt in the energy of my body. All of a sudden, minute energy movements—not just the mental, auditory, and visual cues life gives us—became my information. With practice, I could accurately differentiate what things were causing the movements I was sensing.

What had happened to me that day at the hotel was a profound initiation—or rather, a re-initiation—into a connection I'd had at birth but had learned to ignore or dampen through socialization in our mind-based society. Right or wrong, the reconnection to the shamanic field began to shift my life significantly. I quickly realized and understood the indigenous wisdom that our energy is not ours; it does not belong to us. I recognized that both my energy body and the energy flow within it were connected to the energy of everything around me. I began to live my life in alignment with this overall energy flow, and life became easier—so much easier. It felt like I'd begun to float downstream instead of swimming upstream.

When I asked my teacher, Maria Elena, when in her life she connected with the shamanic field, she said, "I was never disconnected from it. My issue was that I was not connected to the mind. I did not understand the rational-mind perspective." She went on to say that people who are primarily connected to the energy of the body, and thus to the shamanic field, are afraid when someone connected with only the mind is speaking. It frightens them because a mind that is not in communication with the body and its energy field seems, in some ways, to be lying.

I immediately understood what she meant. The reverse is also true: when someone connected only to the mind interacts with people who are connected to the shamanic field via their energy body, those connected to the mind often see the others' actions as illogical and crazy. Yet as irrational as their actions may seem, they are in accord with the larger energy field.

The mind and the body are both worthwhile ways of connecting with the unified energy field. Most people have not trained the mind to be connected either to the unified energy field or to the body and its energy field, so their mind is usually off running wild on its own. Those who follow more mind-full traditions connect to the unified energy field through the mind alone and ignore the information coming from the body. As a result, these people are often connected only through the upper aspects of their body to the unified energy field. For example, they might be able to communicate through what they call angels, to channel spiritual information, or to read the eternal energetic archive of souls known as the Akashic Records; however, they might still be disconnected from temporality, the physical, nature, or the earth—and all the energies these lower aspects of the unified energy field provide. Reading reality at the level of energy requires reading energy through the body. The body is what is connected to the natural world and temporality.

The body is inherently connected to the shamanic field because the energy body is a part of the shamanic field. So if the mind has been trained to listen to and be attuned to the body, voilá, the mind is also connected to the shamanic field. It is possible to connect to the unified field through the upper aspects and the lower parts of our energy body at the same time. Add in connecting through the heart simultaneously, and you are on the fast track to awakening.

The differences in how we connect into the unified field of energy create the dichotomy we see today between traditions. It is the mind-body split, the scientific-indigenous split, some of the yin-yang split, and maybe, in fact, the split between the right and left sides of the brain. Most of us have a penchant for one connection or the other, yet we are all connected in both ways to some extent. I believe that, collectively, we are coming into an integration, into the ability to connect at the mind, the body, and the heart.

With training, the mind can serve the process of connecting to the body and shamanic field; if untrained, the mind can get in the way. I like to use the example of surfing. We are out on our surfboard in life. The water is the shamanic field of energy, and the waves are the experiences and events that come to us in life. A big wave of energy comes, in the form of an event or experience. We have a choice to surf it or not. If the mind says, "This wave should not be here!" we become so distracted that surfing the wave is impossible, and we crash with the wave. If we see the wave of energy coming, we can ride it to the best of our ability until the water becomes calm again. We may still crash, but if we do, we then have a choice: get back on the board and surf, or sit in the water wondering what happened. We are always surfing these energy waves, both in our personal lives and in the collective energy of the shamanic and uni-fied energy fields.

Most people who come through my door do not have a problem understanding the mind and working from that. However, they are often working from a mind that is not strongly connected to the shamanic field or the unified energy field; instead, it is connected only to their own energy field. Because we have often dampened our ability to sense energy and read reality at the level of energy, we are working with only our own field, not tapping into the larger field of awareness. The aperture that allows awareness to come in is too small. In these cases, people are living their lives from a set of ideas about how life should be. There is a lot of disappointment in this disconnected reality. Life is always following the rules of energy, and if we are not connected to these rules, it appears that nothing is happening the "right" way.

Once we connect our personal energy field to the unified field of awareness, then we begin to float downstream, to flow with the current of our life. We begin to have new abilities, new access to awarenesses, and we are capable of action that is outside our old range of possibility. What is "wrong" with our life starts to make sense when we begin following the rules of energy and stop attempting to swim upstream. Sometimes we will realize that what appears to be "not working" is actually happening exactly as it should; it is the appearance that shifts. We can pitch our awareness to the larger field of energy around us, and it augments our perspective on life and healing.

I am not dismissing the mind here. I think the last five hundred years of rational thought have brought wondrous advances to life. I also think that we have become over-domesticated in many ways.

We know from research that animals respond to information outside our normal awareness. During the Southeast Asia tsunami of 2003, many animals moved out of the affected area before the wave hit. Cats in Los Angeles disappear before earthquakes at a predictably high rate. But researchers looking at animals' connections with the seismic field—a vibrational field of the earth and thus part of the shamanic field—have found that animals in zoos have lost the ability to respond to these natural fields. I think the same is true for us. We have lost some of our instinctual responsiveness, and I believe it is a result of disconnecting ourselves from or dampening down the information and vibrations that come to us through our lower chakras or the lower dan tien—the parts of our energy anatomy that naturally connect us to the shamanic field and to the wisdom of the body, earth, and natural world. In some ways we have become over-domesticated like the zoo animals—no longer able to instinctively respond to seismic vibrations or information from the natural world.

Although we may have closed ourselves off to these signals, it is impossible for us to be disconnected from the shamanic field. Because we cannot ever totally lose that connection, it is possible for us to reopen our awareness of it.

REOPENING OUR CONNECTIONS

When I experienced the buzzing in my pelvis, I knew that I was connecting to the unified energy field with my root chakra. Since then, I have come to realize that it is possible to connect to the unified field of energy through any chakra or dan tien. Staying connected to the energy of the mind (via the upper dan tien and upper chakras), the heart (via the middle dan tien or heart chakra), and body (the lower dan tien or lower chakras) can lead us to different experiences of the present moment, because each connects us to a different aspect of the unified energy field. When my root-chakra connection to the unified energy field was reinitiated, I was reopening my ability to experience my body's connection to the shamanic-field aspect of the unified energy field. As we explore the heart center later in the book, you will experience being connected to the unified energy field through the heart, which is also part of its own collective energy field.

It is also possible to be connected to the unified energy field through multiple energy centers in the body at once and, thus, hold two or three or more states of awareness and connection at once. Doing so takes time and practice, and it is an art.

To develop this skill of staying connected, I spent two years listening to my body more than my head. Because the body and cells are more primary to health and healing than the thought processes, I decided to do whatever actions my lower chakras and lower dan tien, the parts of my energy anatomy that registered my body's wisdom and the wisdom of the shamanic field, were aligned with. When I had a choice of what to do, I did what enlivened my lower dan tien.

I began to notice a vibration there that dampened when my head wanted to do an activity but my body didn't. Having followed the call of my mind for the better part of thirty-seven years, I decided to follow the call from my lower dan tien all day long—every time I had to choose between different possibilities.

What I found was surprising—and that is probably no surprise. Often in the mornings when I awoke, my body was not aligned with the plans I had made for that day, and that difference proved to be a challenge. Once, my husband and I had planned a day together. I was excited for the rare time away from the children, alone with my husband. But when I checked in with the lower dan tien, the message I received was, "Go to the pottery studio. Make something creative." I was shocked and wondered how to broach the subject with my husband. When I did, he said he would love to play golf for the morning, and why didn't we then spend the afternoon together? (Perhaps our bodies had already mutually decided what was going to happen. Perhaps I was responding to his body-fullness, or he was already aligned with mine.)

So we spent our morning in our own activities. I went to the pottery studio and began to work with the clay, letting my hands guide the work without any thought to what I was making. I was surprised when I created a sculpture of a woman kneeling, giving birth to a baby. Stunned, I admired her. Four days later, I became pregnant, against many odds. I had used plenty of contraception—in fact, more than usual. (Perhaps I was a bit aware of what my body was planning, because I'd used extra contraception.) The mystery occurred anyway. The sculpture had provided the map, so when I saw the positive pregnancy test a few weeks later, I knew I had been forewarned and was ready. I think my body was connected to the future and to its own desires, despite the fact that my husband and I thought we had completed our family. The sculpture presaged joy, and I was aligned to our next journey through the body. The mind's thought "But I was going to . . ." was quelled because I was following the wisdom of vitality.

When we connect to the unified energy field through the body, it is easy to sense what is coming. We often become less interested in ideas but more connected to what is happening and will happen. We are comfortable letting what sparks us and the pull of the unified energy field run the show—not our mind or our ideas or the minds or ideas of others. I feel that when we are aligned, we get a sense of what is coming and align our energies with it, which then means we now want it. When it appears, it seems like "I just got what I wanted! I manifested it!" This perspective on manifestation differs from that of many teachers. I think we do not actually manifest everything; instead, we are able to sense what is coming into our lives and align with it. When the thing or event occurs, we may feel as if we made it happen, we manifested it, or we got what we wanted, but what we really did is connect with what is already happening and what is due to come. Desire does play a crucial role, as our desire can stimulate the flow of energy to flow toward us. In this sense, we are involved in manifestation. Yet our desire is for life, healing, or vitality, not a new car or more money, for example. Manifestation, then, is actually the ability to be available to the information of the unified energy field, and the shamanic field specifically; to respond to what quickens us through our energy centers; and to be open to whatever is about to occur.

THE ROLE OF TRADITION AND CULTURE IN CONNECTING WITH THE FIELDS

Lydia is a shaman with whom I have spent time in Mexico; she is part of the Seri tribe. The deity of the Seri Indians is the pelican, and historically the Seris made their clothes from pelican skins and feathers. When I asked Lydia how she connects to the shamanic energy field for healing work, she said she connects through the birds.

On one journey in Mexico, Lewis Mehl-Madrona and I brought a group to work with healing ceremonies. Lydia and a few women from her tribe joined us. One of our participants asked Lydia for a healing. Lydia sat down, shook the rattle in her hand, and sang a song to the birds. We were on the second floor of a house, and there was a balcony outside. As Lydia was singing, the balcony outside became full of birds; they were landing and hanging out on the railing, looking inside, drawn to Lydia's strong connection to the bird energy, I am sure. When she finished, the birds flew away. Birds live within the natural world or shamanic field, and Lydia was able to connect specifically to the bird energy because she was part of a culture or healing tradition that revered birds.

Our Western minds do not always see or understand. When Lydia had finished her song, she nodded to me; the healing was done. Our client was lying on the floor and looked confused. When would the healing occur? I understood her confusion, so I leaned over to Lydia and whispered in my poor Spanish, "Lydia, we are the white ones. We must see a healing to feel it has been done. Could you go over to our client here and use your hands to do a healing on her as well?" Lydia smiled and nodded. She walked over to this young woman and ran her hands over her body for a few minutes. Then she nodded again. I thanked her and so did the client, who immediately relaxed and smiled.

Nearly everyone has had experiences of the "invisible world" making contact with them. My grandmother once told me a story about holding my aunt Betsy, a newborn, in her arms. My grandfather was making a repair on the roof, and she was standing outside under the roof where he was working. She told me she heard her dead mother's voice yell, "Mea, step back!" Without thinking, my grandmother immediately stepped back, and just as she did, a hammer accidentally dropped off the roof and barely missed her and her infant.

People whose traditions and culture include spirits of the deceased serving as our guides and mentors might say that my grandmother had actually heard the voice of her dead mother from the "other side." Some people who are connected to the world of spirit guides might say that my grandmother's guides had taken on her mother's voice to get her to move, and others might say the voice she heard was that of God. Still others might say that my grandmother's energy field had noticed the shift of the hammer and alerted her subconscious mind, which gave her a clear signal to move. From the level of energy and the body, what I think happened is this: my grandmother received a vibrational message from the energy field about what was just about to happen. That message came in through her body, stimulated her mothering instinct to protect her child, and was translated into her mother's voice warning her to move. All of this happened at the same instant she stepped back. For someone else, there may not have been a voice, just a step back with no "explanation." All information, whether it comes to us as sound, thought, sensation, insight, intuition, or another channel or form, is actually translated energy. The vibration comes in and is filtered through the assemblage points or chakras or filters that it activates.

How we ask ourselves the question about connection to the invisible forms our experience. Recognizing how we translate the energy of the unified and shamanic fields inside ourselves—as a voice, movement, or impulse—is the trick to beginning to read the fields. It allows us to make sense of little cues and actions that seemingly make no sense. I believe we use our religions, beliefs, and traditions as structures for understanding what I call our *primary awareness*, which is active all the time.

Once an African shaman told me, "You hear all the spirits." I took that to mean that I can listen or read the fields in a primary way, and that means more energy—the energy of the entire unified energy field and all parts of it—is available to me, not only the energy filtered or represented through my own healing tradition. For example, when I am in a new place, the images I receive are often aligned with that culture, even if I do not know about that culture. I think this happens because the images are not separate from the land that culture is based in. If I am listening to the land, it can gift up the images harvested by those who live there. If I limit my hearing to only my tradition, all the vibrations I receive are translated into the images and understandings of that tradition.

When we begin to really listen to the unified field of energy, many new dimensions of it open up. Realizing how we currently translate energetic, vibrational information is key to beginning to track the entire unified field and energy. It bears repeating: our energy is not really ours; it belongs to the larger flow of energy that is the unified energy field. Opening and connecting to the larger unified energy field allows us to feel and connect into vitality, awareness, and healing. Life still happens; we still get sick, injured, or exhausted. Yet if we keep our personal energy field open to the vitality of the energy in the lower body, and if we clear previous blocks and continue to work with the energy, life will lead us to that which we need next. Physical healing is augmented, and certainly we can have more health and vitality. I have seen people stay connected to energy and vitality even as they make their last transition into death.

Reading the unified energy field is a skill and a wondrous advantage that helps us enjoy life. I think everyone can learn to read and listen to it, regardless of whether she or he has the desire, capacity, or calling to be a shaman or healer. Reading the field includes knowing that the energy in it is conscious. It is awareness; it is awake. The unified energy field cannot make a mistake; only our interpretation of it can be off. Reading the field is what is required to deeply explore energy, energy healing, and body awakening, and the body is the best energy reader we have. Toward the end of this book, we will explore how to begin reading the field.

CHAPTER 3

Getting Started: Using Movement to Open, Clear, Ground, and Receive Energy

With passionate practices
I held the reins secure on my mind
And made the breath one column

—Lalla, *Naked Song*

We can now begin to explore the exercises I consider cornerstones for self-healing with the energy flow in the body. We will start by more fully opening and clearing the lower energy centers of the body—the legs, first chakra, second chakra, and lower dan tien—and connecting to the unified energy field through these centers. Opening and clearing these lower centers is important to our well-being because through them we harvest vital energy from the earth's energy field and because it helps us balance the energy within our body.

GATHERING ENERGY

In my medical practice, I have people in their late forties or fifties coming into the office and complaining of chronic exhaustion for the first time in their lives. They are perplexed about why they no longer have the energy and vitality they had when they were younger.

Here is the key to this vitality work: our energy is not ours. It is dependent on how connected we are to the energy field of the earth. Each of us is born with a yolk sac of energy that life gifts to us, but by midlife we have used up this energy. So after the age of forty or so, we must gather energy into our personal energy fields each day. Fortunately, we are part of and, therefore, in constant connection with the energy field of the earth, so we can gather energy from it for ourselves.

The part of our energy anatomy that connects us to this larger field is the lower dan tien or lower chakra centers, in the lower part of the body. Once we tap into the larger energy field of the earth, we feel enlivened and vital; when we are closed off from it because of blocks in our lower energy bodies, we feel tired. Staying vital, creative, responsive, and connected to the energy of the earth starts with keeping the lower energy centers and the channels in the legs and hips open to gather energy and to support and hold the energy we have gathered. Because our connection with the earth's energy field is in constant flux, we often need to clear our lower energy centers multiple times a day initially in order to keep the energy exchange flowing.

The second exercise in this chapter, Full-Body Tapping, is specifically designed to help us gather energy from the earth to stimulate and awaken the body.

GROUNDING

Grounding the body means strengthening our connection between our root chakra or lower dan tien and the shamanic field. Doing so balances the energy flow between the body and the head, ensuring that the bulk of the energy is centered in the body. Grounding the physical body is enormously helpful. Grounding means focusing on the core of our energy body in the lower dan tien and having the legs and hips open to the flow of the energy from the earth.

In our culture, many of us carry the bulk of our energy in our heads, not in our bodies. On the physical level, keeping most of our energy centered upward, in the upper energy centers, can lead to an imbalance of the autonomic nervous system, producing anxiety and an overreactive sympathetic nervous system. For the most part, this upward shift has occurred over the past two hundred to five hundred years. Our culture reveres the mind, and as a whole, we have our energy focused higher in the body—more so than the Seri Indians in Mexico, for example.

Whether this imbalance is caused by stress or is an inadequate response to stress, I do not know. What I do know is that this upward shift of energy is heightened by trauma, such as an accident, an illness, a surgery, a fearful or frightening occurrence, or even just bad news. What we often do in these situations is pull the energy of the pain, trouble, or trauma to our head and think about it in an attempt to solve it, to soften our feelings about it, to help ourselves in the moment, or to prevent it from happening again. Shifting the energy of the experience upward and away from the lower portion of the physical body pulls us out of balance at the level of the energy body, resulting in ungroundedness or *asustado*. This Spanish word means "frightened" or "scared" and is a common diagnosis made by energy healers in Mexico. I see this condition in clients who have gone through a difficult time, become hurt or sick, or experienced a shocking or painful event. In response, their energy body has pulled up and away from the lower portion of the physical body. The resulting situation resembles depression. These people experience a generalized low level of energy. They have a hard time making decisions, they can't understand why, and there is no energy to fix the situation.

After my third child was born, I was wildly ungrounded. I had just undergone a C-section, and a week later, my other two children were in a minor auto accident. I was a mess; I could not make a decision, I cried frequently, and I felt very depressed. I wondered if I was experiencing postpartum depression and whether the root of postpartum depression was being ungrounded or unbalanced.

I had planned a healing journey to Mexico for myself and my two-month-old baby. I could not decide whether to go, nor could I even pack for the trip. It was as if I were paralyzed from inside. I could not even decide what type of milk to buy at the grocery store. I managed to board the two of us on the plane to Mexico, but when a friend who was also on the plane mentioned that she was glad I had decided to come, I responded, "Oh, I don't think I'm going on the trip." She inquired gently, "When do you think you will decide to go?" This is how disconnected I was from my root chakra, my energy body, and my temporal reality.

This waffling went on for three days after we'd landed in Cancun, until I saw a lovely Mexican healer. In the middle of the healing session, I felt and heard a clunk in my lower pelvis. My energy became regrounded and returned to alignment. Within the hour, I was fully in the moment. I could make decisions, was aligned with being on the journey, and felt I was back to myself.

That was my first embodied experience with this depth of being ungrounded. I believe this asustado has happened to me many times and continues to happen in my life in smaller ways, yet that particular asustado experience was a teacher. Since then, I have had clients who have described feeling the same clunk during a healing session without knowing about the energy body or about being ungrounded.

I see symptoms of asustado in our culture on a large scale. Whenever I believe someone's symptoms are the result of asustado, I have the client do as many grounding exercises as possible, including the two exercises described next in this chapter—Toe Tapping and Shaking the Bones—as well as Foot Tapping and the Root Chakra Breath (described in later chapters). Using these exercises to bring the physical body back into alignment with the energy body can almost immediately alleviate the symptoms of asustado. If the symptoms have been present for a long time, more prolonged grounding exercises may be needed. For example, if someone had a car accident five years before and has experienced low-level depression since, it may take six months of working with the exercises to fully reground the body. Further, the practices help with grounding the body enough so asustado doesn't happen as often. We can use the body to train ourselves to stop pulling everything up to the head and experience the event that has caused the fright or shock.

TOE TAPPING

Toe tapping is an ancient practice that opens the energy flow in the legs and hips and aligns the energy body in the lower portion of the physical body. Toe tapping also helps balance the energy between the body and head, while it dramatically stimulates energy flow in the legs, allowing you to become connected to the larger energy field of the earth.

Toe tapping affects many aspects of health. From a traditional Chinese medicine point of view, it stimulates the spleen, liver, and stomach channels; these are the energy meridians that are responsible for overall energy flow, vitality, and blood flow.[1] Toe tapping also stimulates the lymphatic flow in the legs, the venous return of blood to the heart, and the nerve signals in the legs and hips. It is useful for helping restless leg syndrome, insomnia, and neuropathic pain. Because it is so grounding, it is also remarkable for treating anxiety. One can use this exercise to stem a panic attack, and it's often easier to do than a mindfulness exercise or a breathing technique, because during a panic or anxiety attack, the breath and mind are often in chaos.

Toe tapping is an adaptogen that will get the body back into balance. This exercise can energize you when energy is low and relax you when you are wired or anxious. It will get your energy going for the day and help you fall asleep at night.

Before You Start

You will need to find a comfortable place on the floor. If you have back problems, you can do this exercise lying on a bed or a couch. *Do not do this exercise if you have had a recent knee or hip replacement or if you are pregnant.* If you've had recent knee or hip replacement, you may use a handheld vibrating massager to stimulate flow in the feet and legs; rub the massager all over your feet and legs to simulate the Toe Tapping. There are meridian points in the legs and hips that can stimulate labor, so pregnant women should wait until after birth to do the exercise or use the massager. There will be other exercises in this book that will safely open your legs and hips if you are pregnant.

If you have had injuries in the legs and pelvis, you may notice some pain or discomfort. If you do, you can continue the exercise and work through it. If it becomes really uncomfortable, just stop

TOE TAPPING

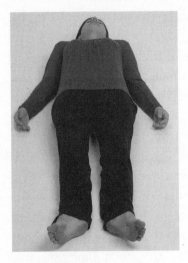

Figure 12a: Starting position for Toe Tapping.

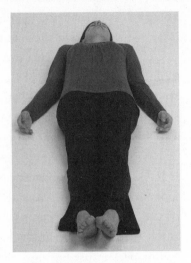

Figure 12b: Leave your heels in place, rotate your legs inward from your hips, and tap your big toes together.

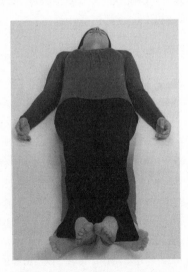

Figure 12c: Rotate your legs inward and outward from the hips, letting momentum keep the movement going.

and do the exercise later, shortening the duration so that you can allow the flow of blocked energy to repair itself gently over time. Just about everyone will notice some pain in the big toes and a little burning in their thighs. This effect is normal; just work through it, and it will diminish in the first few minutes of the practice.

The Practice

The key to this exercise is that the legs rotate from the hips, much like windshield wipers on a car. Find a comfortable place on the floor or your bed. Lie flat on your back. Allow your hips and legs to rest easily, hips loose and feet apart. Rotate or rock your legs and feet, in and out from your hips, leaving your heels in one place on the floor. If you notice your heels slipping, wear socks or put a yoga mat under your feet to keep them from slipping side to side. Now roll your legs, first tapping your big toes together and then letting your legs and feet roll back out. Keep your legs straight. Make sure that you are rotating your legs from the hips, not just from the ankles. Begin to tap your big toes together quickly. (See figures 12a, 12b, and 12c.)

The faster you tap, the easier it will be to do this exercise, because you will be using momentum from the previous tap as well as the rotator muscles in your hips and thighs. Any discomfort in your toes and thighs will pass in a few minutes.

Close your eyes and relax. Listening to fast, rhythmic music helps, because you can tap to the beat. Continue the tapping for five minutes at first, then work up to longer periods. I like doing this exercise for twenty minutes or longer, depending on how much time I have.

Once you stop, rest on your back. Notice how you feel and relax in this position for a moment. Where is your awareness in your body at this moment? Become aware of how you feel in your feet, legs, pelvis, torso, arms, hands, chest, and head.

When to Use Toe Tapping

Use this exercise daily in the morning to open the energy flow in the lower portion of your body. You may also use it at night if you have difficulty with insomnia or restless leg syndrome, as it will settle your energy flow and allow you to sleep. This practice deepens and shifts the energy body with time; you will become quite comfortable with it. Give it at least a month. Do not be surprised if you fall in love with it once you get the rhythm of it.

I consider this exercise one of the mainstays of an anxiety-treatment program. It affects the flow of energy in the body as well as the autonomic nervous system, which is responsible for our fight-or-flight response—the part of the nervous system that causes anxiety and panic. Patients often burst into my office a month after starting Toe Tapping and tell me, "It worked! I began to have anxiety, I tapped, and it went away!"

I mention a month here for a reason. When anxiety begins, the autonomic nervous system fires, and you are then in a state of anxiety. The anxiety is hard to shift, and you just have to go along for the ride. However, if you use a practice like this when you are not anxious, the body will get used to the balance the practice provides. After time, the body will cue you to toe tap when anxiety begins, but you have to practice it for at least a month. With time, the body begins rebalancing, and it will point you toward rebalancing when needed. Remember, the body moves toward wholeness and healing; once you get these pathways started, the body will begin to long for the work when it is needed. Then you won't have to remember to use Toe Tapping for anxiety. If you do the exercise enough when it is easy, it will become a natural response when you need it.

FULL-BODY TAPPING

With Toe Tapping, we can open the channels to the lower half of the body. This next exercise, Full-Body Tapping, brings energy up from the earth to the energy reservoir in the lower dan tien, in the abdomen, and moves it from there to stimulate and awaken the body. Energy blocks begin to dissolve as we tap in specific areas of the body.

The practice starts with tapping on the lower dan tien to build energy for the day. If you have limited time, tap on the lower dan tien and on the hips for a quick energy gathering, but I encourage you to take time to tap on the entire body because doing so stimulates more energy flow. You can do this practice fifteen minutes or longer, even up to an hour.

Today there are multiple popular techniques for tapping on specific points on the body. These are wonderful, yet I prefer tapping on the whole body. I have seen this exercise move energy in the sinuses, shoulders, legs, and even in the abdomen. It helps with physical and emotional blockages. It is wonderful, and you will quickly learn where you need to do more tapping.

Before You Begin

If you are pregnant, skip the belly-tapping portion of this exercise. If you have pain in the knees, sway from side to side instead of bouncing up and down. If you cannot tap on all areas because of a physical disability, use a handheld massager.

At the end of this exercise, we will tap on the back. If you do not have someone who can do this for you, use a handheld massager.

The Practice

Do this exercise standing. You may keep your feet a bit farther apart than your normal stance for balance.

We start with the second chakra and lower dan tien, above the pubic bone and below the navel, right on the bladder (figure 13a). Make soft fists and tap on this area while you bounce gently with your knees to pump energy up through your legs. This can be a small motion as long as you move up and down. Breathe into your lower abdominal area while you work here. Pick a spot on the floor and focus your eyes on it to help keep the awareness in your body. Tap here for two to three minutes. Next tap around your abdomen, following in a clockwise circular path, for another minute. Then stand still and see whether you can feel the energy that has gathered for the day. It may feel like a swirling or heat. Don't worry if you don't feel anything. I didn't begin to feel the energy until I had practiced this exercise for a month.

Resume bouncing and move your hands to the lung area and tap the entire chest area with the hands or fingertips (figure 13b). This is a wonderful place to tap if you have lung problems or grief. Try using your fingertips, your whole hands, or your fists to see which works best. Remember to be gentle with yourself in the beginning.

Now tap on your left armpit with your palm. Tapping on the armpits is important for easing depression and relieving problems in the shoulder, arm, wrist, and hand.

Continue by tapping down the left arm. Move down the arm slowly, and spend a little extra time anywhere you notice discomfort. When you reach the left hand, clap your hands together briefly. This will stimulate all the energy points in the hands. Then tap back up the left arm, visiting any places you did not tap on the way down. I tap down one side of the arm and hand and back up the other.

Do the same with your right arm, beginning at the armpit and then working down and back up the right arm.

Using both hands, tap the back of the neck and shoulders with your fingertips. This is a spot where many people carry stress, so tapping here is helpful for neck and arm problems and headaches. Tap up the back of the head, over the crown, and then on the sides of the head.

Figure 13a: Begin Full-Body Tapping by making soft fists and tapping on the lower dan tien.

Figure 13b: Continue Full-Body Tapping by tapping the entire chest area with your fists or fingertips.

Next, with your fingertips, tap on your forehead, down your face, and over the cheekbones. If you have sinus problems, spend extra time over your cheeks and forehead.

Move to the jaw and tap. This is a wonderful way to move energy in your jaw if you have temporomandibular joint (TMJ) pain.

Tap down the front of the neck to the top of the chest.

Now move to the hips. With your fists, tap on the front of the hips where the legs meet the body. Tap on both the right and the left hip at the same time. I think these points are very important. They are the gates where the energy we gather from the earth enters the upper body, and tapping on them is important for treating leg pain, hip problems, restless leg syndrome, leg edema, vascular (blood-flow) problems in the legs, and overall energy flow.

Move to the sacrum or tailbone. The sacrum is another important gate in the energy body, and it needs to be cleared often. Tapping on the sacrum is important if you have any kind of back pain. Move to tapping on the buttocks. We sit so frequently that this area often needs energy movement.

Pause for a moment and stand still. Now you'll begin tapping down and back up the legs. Start with the left leg; with both hands open, tap down your left leg. On the way back up the leg, visit any places you did not tap on the way down. I like to tap the front and outside of the leg on the way down and the back and inside on the way up. Spend extra time on the outer portion of the thighs if you are tight there. Pain is an indication of blocked energy, so tap more on any place with discomfort. Move to the right leg and tap down and back up in the same pattern.

When you have finished the right leg, stop tapping, stand up, and close your eyes. Check in with your body. How does your body feel? Is there any area that needs more work? If so, spend time tapping wherever you feel you need more work.

Finally, your back needs to be cleared. Have another person tap in the center of your back, between the shoulder blades. If no one is with you, use a handheld massager. Spend at least two minutes on the center of the back to clear it. Then you can move to tapping on the rest of the back for another two minutes. Again, spend extra time on any parts of the back that you sense may need more work.

Stand still, close your eyes, and notice how you feel.

When to Use Full-Body Tapping

Use Full-Body Tapping any time you want to energize your body. It can be a daily or weekly practice, depending on how much time you can allow in the morning. It's also wonderful for recharging yourself in the afternoon. You may use it with any illness, as it will address energy blocks in all areas of your body.

I adjust this exercise according to need. For example, if I feel a cold coming on, I will tap longer on my sinus area and chest. Once, at an intensive workshop, I had a client with a thirty-year history of chronic sinusitis. While we did many activities with her over four days, we spent extra time tapping on the face in our morning practice. Her sinuses cleared on the last day of the intensive and stayed clear for two and a half years. When I saw her again after this, she mentioned that the chronic sinusitis had returned—after she had stopped the face tapping. I advised her to begin again, and again her sinuses cleared.

Full-Body Tapping is a wonderful practice to do in a group. If you want to learn more about using this practice in a group, visit a center for Dahn Yoga, a type of yoga that includes body tapping and some of the other energy healing exercises in this book.

SHAKING THE BONES

Emotion is actually energy in motion (e-motion), and every experience we have carries its own energy to be experienced. This is a crucial point in healing at the level of the energy body. When we experience our emotions and experiences fully, the energy of both will move all the way through the body, from root to crown chakra, and then either exit through the crown chakra or turn and cycle down the back. Yet a lot of the time, we pull the energy to the head and begin to think about it, actually changing the natural flow of energy through the body. When that happens, the energy crystallizes in the body and can continue to pop up in our awareness as a memory over and over again. When we clear energy blocks in the body, what we are really doing is clearing the energy of old illness, old trauma, old feelings, and old experiences—old somaticized or stored energies.

Sometimes, when we begin to clear the body, old feelings or experiences may pop up. It is good when this happens. We want this to happen. But when it does, don't bring the energy of that feeling or experience up to the head. Instead, use the following practice, Shaking the Bones, to move it all the way through your energy body and out of it.

Shaking the Bones is the best exercise I know for clearing our energy body and revitalizing our physical body. Animals shake off experiences to clear themselves of the energy of that experience, and then they can move on without having a residual or post-traumatic experience of events. Once I saw a man viciously kick a dog. The dog yelped in pain, shook off the experience, and then walked down the street relaxed, as if nothing had happened. We can see this energy clearing with domesticated pets. Watch a cat or dog shake its body after a fall, a jump, or a surprising experience. It shakes out the experience and moves on to a state of relaxation. In our culture, we even use the phrase "shaking it off" to describe this action.

While you're doing this exercise, you may notice strong feelings—grief, memories, or even joy—come into your awareness. That's a point of this exercise. Don't think about what has come up; just shake it out. Use your breath to clear the experience or the feeling as you shake it out with movement. Most feelings will move through in a few minutes.

Before You Begin

You will need a place to stand on the floor and music with a fast beat. Any music with a good beat—music that you can shake to—will help you shake for a longer period of time. I use the music of James Asher from his album *Shaman Drums*.[2] I like the song titled "Amma" to start this exercise.

The Practice

We do this exercise standing. Imagine a cord going from the crown of your head up to the sky, and relax your body like a rag doll. Let your neck go limp and your head drop forward. Close your eyes.

As the music plays, vigorously shake your arms and your body, and bounce gently at your knees. The head hangs forward and moves with the body; let it roll slowly from side to side (see figure 14). Let the movement, your breath, and the music take over, and allow yourself to let go. If at any point this exercise becomes difficult or intense, open your eyes, stop shaking, and stand still.

Do this Shaking the Bones for at least five minutes. Ten or fifteen minutes is even more effective.

Stop and notice how you feel.

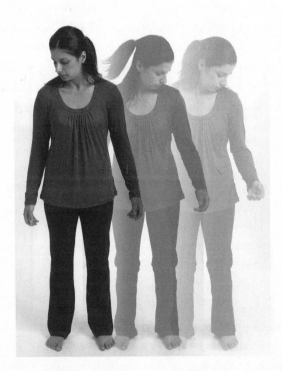

Figure 14: For Shaking the Bones, bounce up and down gently at your knees while vigorously shaking your arms and your body. The head hangs forward; let it roll slowly from side to side as your body moves.

When to Use Shaking the Bones

I suggest you use Shaking the Bones first thing in the morning or any time after you've had a difficult experience or even a difficult conversation. You can also use this exercise at the end of the day to clear away the day and prepare for a new one, or to clear any old experiences you've had.

Each time you do this exercise, it will be different and will deepen what's happening in your body and in your life. You may find that you want to use this practice for longer periods of time with certain circumstances, like very difficult experiences or traumas from the distant past.

When I received the news that my father was dying, as a physician I immediately went to my head to think about any medications I could suggest to keep him alive. I knew that going to my head was a level of defense. I needed instead to feel the authentic experience of a daughter losing her father. I went to my office and started to do Shaking the Bones. It took me about twenty minutes to shed all the overlying story in order to get to the underlying authentic feeling. This exercise helped me tremendously. When I went to visit my father, I did not waste energy on changing or fixing him or on the medical process. I was able to greet my dying father.

Practice these three energy-movement exercises daily to begin to experience differently the energy of the body and the energy around you. This is experiential wisdom; using the practices will open you to the experience of the energy in the body being connected to a larger field.

CHAPTER 4

The Heart Center
and the Art of Sacred Touch

I came to the door and saw how
Powerfully the locks were bolted
And the longing in me became that strong
And then I saw that I was gazing
From within the presence

—Lalla, *Naked Song*

We are going to shift now from connecting to the earth's energy field through the lower body to connecting into our energy body and the unified field of energy through the heart center. We call this energy center the heart center because it spans traditions and the differences in energy anatomies between the traditions. It is an important assemblage point whether we look at it as part of the matrix tradition, as the Hindu heart chakra, or as the middle dan tien from traditional Chinese medicine (TCM).

The heart center, located in the chest, is the most important energy center for healing work. The energy that is generated, amplified, and filtered by the heart center is intrinsically healing. When any form of healing is chorded to the energy of the heart center, it has an amazing ability to transform.[1] By *chorded*, I mean holding two states of consciousness or awareness at once. While we can perform healing from our normal awareness, if we chord the heart-center energy to our work, we are using energy healing techniques at the same time that we are focusing on the energy of the heart center. Holding both points of awareness takes practice, but how you do it will become more apparent as you travel through this book.

When focused, the transpersonal love energy of the heart center can give clarity to a healing dynamic, a personal dynamic, or an event much more quickly than the energy of the other chakras can. The energy of the lower chakras (root and second chakras) has a big impact on healing, yet the heart center is the pinnacle of transformation. Just as the root and second chakra energies are the most important for ongoing vitality, the heart center is the most important for healing.

The heart-center energy is healing for the mind as well as for the body. How we view the world affects how we perceive the experiences that happen to us. When we view the world over and over through the same filters, such as the filter of "me and mine," we can end up with repetitive thoughts and views that no longer serve our circumstances or life and that can drain our vitality and energy field. Some of our thoughts, especially repeating thoughts or thought forms, are just reflections of the energies moving through the body, or patterns of stored or stagnant energy in the body that continue to be reflected up to the mind. In other words, much of the worry and anxiety we experience stems from an unbalanced energy body, which affects our thoughts, which affect our nervous system, which then affects our mind. The thoughts aren't primary; the body is. Exploring the heart center allows us another perspective on any event or reality we are living. Working with the heart center long term can allow this to become one of our primary assemblage points through which to constellate reality.

DEEPER INTO THE TRANSPERSONAL NATURE OF THE HEART CENTER

It is the transpersonal nature of healing that brings about the most change, and the heart center is a transpersonal source of love and energy.

Often when we think we are working from our heart, we are really working with love from a place of personal preference. Personal preference is formed in the third chakra, a place of differentiating self and other ("me or mine"). The third chakra is important; without it, we would not be able to determine "This is me, not you." This differentiation is critical for survival. Most of the loving relationships in our lives are *personal* relationships based in the realm of the third chakra—ego differentiation and "This is me, and that is you." As such, they are not solely unconditional. They come from the level of personal preference and "This is how it should be." We teach our children according to personal love, to socialize them into society.

By contrast, the heart center is a transpersonal source of love. It is the source and connection into the unified field at the level of love—unattached, unconditional, pure love, in whatever form love may look like. Transpersonal love does not always look pleasant. It can be fierce, passionate, destructive; it can have many faces or presentations. The heart center can encompass an understanding or reverence for everything—from the terrific to horrific. Parenthood; close, loving relationships; spirituality; and large or traumatic life events can bring us to the energy and love of heart center—so long as we do not live through our children's accomplishments, the relationship, the spiritual teachings, or the life-changing event as a way to feel our own power or sense of importance through their world.

The heart center is not about personal preference, nor is it is about accepting everything that comes our way. The heart center's energy is a collective energy that allows for the reverence of all life. To fully understand this, you have to practice the Heart Center Meditation to kindle and experience the specific quality of the heart-center energy.

There is a pair of wonderful teachings that begins to explain the difficulty in the differentiating between the personal preference or personal love of the third chakra and the transpersonal, universal love of the heart center: "The cave of a thousand years ends in the heart," and "The path of a thousand miles ends in the heart." It takes time to understand this small shift to the heart center. "A thousand years" or "a thousand miles" refers to the work of centering over and over in the heart center before this differentiation is clear or apparent. What we normally think of as love is rooted in personal preference, and it is necessary. But for healing work, we need to move to unconditional love and reverence for all that is, including any disease, illness, or past experience we are working with. We need to learn this path away from personal preference to the heart center. It is a discipline to feel a personal preference and then shift to the heart center for a different view. While shifting states of consciousness from the personal preference to the heart center can be challenging initially, the best way to explore this shift is by practicing the Heart Center Meditation often enough that we can shift to the heart center quickly when we need to. To do that, we will move into a heart center meditation, a direct experience of the heart center, later in this chapter.

It is the unconditional love (or energy) of the heart center that is able to see and accept each thing as it is. The heart center contains awe for the mystery of energy and life itself. Although it has different names, the energy of the heart center is present in all religions and spiritual traditions. The energy of the heart is universal; all cultures and religions have a relationship with this energy and practices to stimulate it. Whatever our training or tradition, we all know, at one level, what the energy of the heart center is.

THE ENERGY OF THE HEART

The energy of the heart center is an electromagnetic or vibrational field of the heart, and the heart center is the underlying field of the actual physical heart. The two influence each other the same way the energy body influences the entire physical body. Our overall energy field responds to and serves the heart center first and the other energy centers second.

The Institute of HeartMath has documented that the electromagnetic field of the heart is the strongest in the body overall and specifically for concordance and entrainment.[2] *Concordance* is the synchronization between cardiac function, respiratory rate, and the autonomic nervous system. *Entrainment* is the concept that we are transmitting energetic information via our energy field, consciously and unconsciously, to others and to the environment around us all the time. Entrainment affects our autonomic nervous system, especially our fight-or-flight reaction. The concept of entrainment is well demonstrated in music. In music, one string of an instrument vibrating at one frequency can affect another string, bringing the second string into a harmonic vibration. In the same way, when I teach clients how to toe tap or meditate, I do the exercise with them, and in doing so, I actually transmit the vibration of the experience to them.

Another wonderful story of my friend Keith, whom you met in chapter 1, exemplifies entrainment. Keith had learned how to use movement and sound to move energy and heal his debilitating TMJ. Because he was so in touch with the movements his body had showed him, he would automatically begin to move his neck in a bobbing sort of way, unwinding, when he was relaxing. His neck would move, and his head would tilt from side to side, making a movement that looked like a figure eight or infinity sign. One day, when I picked up Keith at the airport, he mentioned that he thought he had been asleep on the flight, but when he came to, he realized he must have been in a deep state of relaxation instead. When he opened his eyes, he noticed that the man next to him, who was working on his laptop, was moving his head in a figure-eight formation. And the man across the aisle, reading a book, was doing the same thing! Keith also relayed to me that while he was at the bank the week before, he had closed his eyes and relaxed for a moment, unconsciously moving his head this same way. When he opened his eyes, both his wife and the loan officer were doing the same neck movement, completely unaware.

How or why other people were picking up on Keith's movement is the mystery of entrainment. We are transmitting energetic, vibrational information all the time, and that information is far more important than anything we say. What we entrain, regardless of what we are saying (or in conjunction with what we are saying, if our words are of the same vibration), is effective and powerful communication. In fact, great teachers transmit most of their work vibrationally through entrainment, even though their students, at the beginning, think the teaching is coming to them through the words coming out of the teacher's or guru's mouth. Brugh Joy, one of my teachers, used to say that if you want to learn something from someone, be around that person as much as you can. The activity does not matter; just being in his or her presence is enough. The same is true if you want to heal from illness. I counsel my patients to spend time with people who healed from the illness they are struggling with. Survivors have an energetic and physical map at the primary level of pattern that they can transmit, whether they are aware of it or not, through presence and entrainment.

So when we say that the heart is the strongest energy field for entrainment, it means the heart has the capacity to entrain other people around us into its energy field more quickly and more effectively than any other center or electromagnetic field of the body. Like the other passengers on Keith's flight and his wife and the loan officer at the bank, other energy fields will pick up on the energetic vibrations of the heart center and begin to vibrate in the same way.

The heart entrains the brain. "When we focus attention on our hearts, the synchronization between our hearts and brains increases," writes Doc Childre and Howard Martin in their 1999 book, *The Heartmath Solution*. "Experiments suggest that the energetic interaction between the heart and brain plays a part in this process."[3]

The fact that the heart is the strongest field for entrainment is important for healing ourselves and others. The researchers at the Institute of HeartMath have documented that the heart contains an "intelligence" and that "the energetic information contained in the heart's field isn't detected only by our brains and bodies but can also be registered by those around us."[4] This means that when we send heart-center energy to other parts of our body—a kidney, a knee, the lungs—the individual energy fields of those parts will register the heart's energy and attune themselves to it. This also means that when we send heart-center energy through our energy field to others, their energy fields will register this energy and automatically adjust to harmonize with it.

The Institute of HeartMath also has data on *global coherence*, which occurs when a large group tunes in to the heart center's energy. The result is measurable in the group's collective energy field. The Institute also collects data on even larger effects of global coherence, and the data shows that one large group tuning into the heart-center field can have an impact on the measurable energy of the global energy field. Thus, the heart center has a profound impact both in our personal lives and in the larger unified field of energy that we are in constant connection with. The energy of the heart center is powerful medicine for ourselves and the people around us.

THE FOUR ATTRIBUTES OF THE HEART CENTER

When we first begin to actively connect to and explore the energy of the heart center, it's helpful to connect to its attributes. The Western mind needs words or attributes in order to connect to certain energies; words allow us to begin our journey into these universal and collective energies. When we meditate on words that capture the attributes of the heart center, we entrain our energy bodies to the vibrations of those attributes and the center as a whole.

The heart center has four main attributes: compassion, innate harmony, healing presence, and unconditional love.

Compassion

The word *compassion* is from Latin and means "suffering with." Compassion is the loving desire to alleviate another person's suffering, combined with deep respect for that person's experience. It means that we hold the experience *with* the person, alongside, instead of trying to change the experience in order to help him or her feel better. In compassion we touch the truth that all of life, including painful or difficult parts, is sacred. Compassion can be transformed into many things, but it is not pity or feeling sorry for someone. It is tapping into a deep ocean of feeling (including but not limited to pain and suffering)—an ocean that is transpersonal and can be shared between individuals.

Just as there are collective energy fields or vibrations for each of the chakras, there are collective vibrational fields of many other things, including grief, joy, and rage, as well as sexuality, chaos, or turmoil. (Even different illnesses can have their own specific vibrational energy fields.) Have you noticed that when you go to a comedy club to watch a good comedian, by the end of the show it matters little what he or she is saying? Everyone laughs no matter what comes out of the performer's mouth because we've gotten caught up in the vibrational energy field of laughter.

Innate Harmony

Innate harmony is the state of being that encompasses calm in the midst of chaos. This is the still point inside of us, the internal eye of the hurricane. It is a total calm, no matter what is happening in external reality. We have to return to it over and over. Practicing moving to innate harmony is helpful not only to quiet an inner emotional storm or a chaotic mind, but also because during times of difficulty or chaos (including illness), this is the attribute for inner support. Innate harmony provides stabilization during tumultuous or difficult times, if you ever find yourself in an emergency situation or a period of collective or group hysteria.

A friend in the medical field, and a fellow heart-center practitioner, shared a story about innate harmony with me a few years back. One morning she received a call from her husband's running partner saying that her healthy, vibrant husband had just dropped to the ground during their run. My friend worked in cardiology, so she knew that this was very bad news and that her husband probably would not survive this event. As she drove to the hospital to meet the ambulance and discover the outcome of her husband's heart attack, she heard over and over, "Innate harmony, innate harmony, innate harmony." It was an inner chant that carried her through the drive until she reached the hospital. How many times have we heard similar stories of the calm that takes over someone during a crisis, so that he or she is able to do whatever action is required and wait to fall apart afterward? Innate harmony is the heart attribute that allows this to happen. It comes naturally for many people, and with practice, each of us can open our access to this energy in difficult times.

All four attributes of the heart center are innate in the body and innate in the energy field. They come forth when they are needed. Practicing the Heart Center Meditation later in this chapter makes it easier to access them when we need them—in times of healing, crisis, or turmoil. Practice also makes the attributes easier to access with our ordinary awareness on a daily basis.

Healing Presence

Healing presence is the longing and desire toward healing. When I say "toward healing," what I mean is that the longing and desire moves energy toward, or in the direction of, healing. Healing presence is love in action. The body is wired to heal itself, and much of this impulse comes from the energy of healing presence. Healing occurs in the presence of love and the desire for healing.

In the deeper Buddhist teachings, the beginning energy of all creation is within a void. The same is true for the Yaqui and the Seri tribes' worldviews. In fact, it is true in most creation mythologies. The first movement of the energy in this void is love, in the form of healing presence, which then moves the energy of the void toward action, toward the manifestation of the entire universe or reality. This movement of energy to manifestation is the underlying pattern in the unified field of energy, our individual energy body, and our physical bodies and psyches; it is happening all the time. Compassion is then manifested from this movement of love in action toward healing.

All four aspects of the heart center are involved in healing. However, healing presence is the aspect of the heart-center energy that moves and pulls the entire field of energy toward healing, because it actually desires healing and, through love, enacts it.

Unconditional Love

Unconditional love is a radiance of love that is both unconditioned and unconditional. It is divine love or love that comes from a source beyond ourselves; it is an energy from the unified field of energy around us, and we can tap into it. It is also the energy field of love that surrounds us and runs through us. Unconditional love encompasses the ability to appreciate each and every thing exactly as it is, from creation to destruction, exactly as it is. Unconditional love can view each thing or event with reverence for the part it plays in life. It is the shift from judgment to *wow* and *awe*. We do not live from this place of unconditional love moment to moment, as we are individuals with different journeys and personal preferences, yet experiencing unconditional love daily allows for deeper healing than any other energy or meditative state I have experienced.

When people are confused about the transpersonal nature of the heart center or unconditional love, I like to use nature as the ultimate example. Winter comes every year and kills off the leaves and flowers of perennial plants. Can you imagine what would happen if the natural world were upset every time winter came to prune it back and put the plants through their natural cycle of dormancy and regrowth? Unconditional love enables us to we see winter's action for what it is: an inherent, vital aspect of nature.

Visiting the heart center, especially when we are practicing self-healing with energy, allows us easier access to this healing, compassionate, centered, unconditional perspective. It stimulates the body's healing response and shifts old or recent emotional or psychological wounds, because the heart center is what fuels healing in the first place.

I move to the heart center before I place my hands on another person or on myself in a healing mode, because when I do, the quality of energy that I transmit is different than ordinary touch. The hands are fueled by the vibration of the heart center. This happens naturally for many of us; our hands "turn on" when we want to help, serve, assist, or care for ourselves or another in the energy of healing and unconditional love.

THE HEART CENTER MEDITATION

The Heart Center Meditation is my primary form of meditation, even though I have been a student and practitioner of multiple other forms of meditation. This daily meditation practice will help clear your energy body and infuse it with healing energy. The heart center is the wellspring of healing energy. Using this meditation practice daily will accelerate the benefits of healing from exercises in this book.

The placement of the hands during this meditation is important. The hands run energy into the heart center while we meditate. You may have seen paintings or sculptures of the Buddha or other religious figures with their hands in distinctive positions, such as palm up with thumb and middle finger touching. These are mudras, hand positions that move energy and balance energy in the body, and the different positions have specific effects in the body. In this case, the heart-center mudra augments the meditation dramatically. Once you're familiar with the meditation, you can try moving your hands to other locations while practicing it to see how doing so shifts the meditation. Then bring your hands back to your heart chakra and see if you experience any changes in your meditation.

Head position also influences the flow of energy and your focus during meditation. Try tilting your head in different ways and to find a position that helps bring you into the deepest meditative state.

Figure 15 is an illustration of the hand position used in this meditation to connect with your heart center and augment the flow of energy. Place your right hand over your heart area, above your sternum, between the breasts. Place your left hand over your right hand, thumbs touching. If you experience any difficulty maintaining the position as illustrated, try gently pressing your hands into your chest. In the beginning, you can also prop your elbows up with pillows. This hand position becomes effortless over time, so stay with it.

Many people I teach say this is the easiest meditation they have done or that it was the first meditation they were ever able to do. I think this is because the Heart Center Meditation spans multiple forms of meditation with its four attributes. The Heart Center Meditation includes a generative component (creating feeling—in this case, compassion); a receptive component (receiving what is happening—in this case, unconditional love); a Zen-like component, creating a quiet mind (innate harmony); and an active or healing meditation (healing presence). Because it spans multiple forms of meditation, people usually can find their way into the meditation through the attribute or form of meditation they are most akin to. Practice all four attributes when you meditate. Over time, the other attributes will open up as well.

This can be a stationary or a moving meditation. There is movement in the heart center, and I encourage you to move your body if you feel movement while you are meditating. Because the heart is the focus, move your body as you need to for comfort.

Before You Start

Find a comfortable, quiet place to sit. You may want to keep the heart-center attributes written down beside you so that you can look at them until you can recall all four without effort.

If you like music, find a piece that suggests the heart center to you and play it during your meditation. I like the CD *Heart Chakra*

Figure 15: For the Heart Center Meditation, place your right hand over your heart area. Place your left hand over the right, thumbs touching. This hand position is a mudra, moving and balancing energy in the body during the meditation.

Meditation by Karunesh, which has four very similar pieces of music: "North," "East and West," "South," and "Circle."[5] You may meditate to one, two, three, or all four, depending on the length of your meditation. Whatever you choose, I suggest you use the same piece of music each time you meditate—a piece of music you use only for this meditation. Using the same piece of music exclusively will allow you to instinctively move into the heart center as the music begins. The music will become an initiator for the meditation and the state of consciousness you are exploring.

The Practice

Sit in a comfortable position. Place your hands over your heart chakra and close your eyes. Invite in each attribute for the meditation. Focus using image, word, and feeling to stimulate and invoke each attribute in the mantra.

Compassion: Oceanic, limitless compassion.

Innate Harmony: Calm in the midst of chaos, the still point. Infinite, still, bliss.

Healing Presence: Longing and desire toward healing. Love in action.

Unconditional Love: Unconditioned, unconditional love. Reverence. Awe. *Wow.*

Then focus internally on the heart, your breath, and the four attributes. Move if you feel movement. Some people notice a circular movement, or they find that they need to shift position from time to time. Trust that your body is a mudra too; if it wants to move, assist it in moving to a place of comfort.

When to Use the Heart Center Meditation

Meditate for five to twenty minutes daily. If you use the meditation for only five minutes a day, do one twenty-minute Heart Center Meditation each week as well.

DAILY PRACTICE

I want to emphasize the need for a daily practice of self-healing and centering. Healing and homeostasis of the energy body and physical body is a constant process, occurring in each moment, so do not make your self-healing practice only a once-a-week or once-a-month event. A daily practice will keep the flow of energy clear and will continue to encourage and facilitate the energy body and physical body to heal themselves. Just as we take in water and food daily, we can work with our own body daily for healing. Use the self-healing practices every day to receive the fullest benefit of the work you are doing with yourself.

A daily practice should include both a movement component and a meditative component. I find that if I use a movement practice first, then my meditation goes much deeper. I like to use one of the energy-gathering, grounding, or clearing exercises first (see chapter 3) and the Heart Center Meditation second. I suggest that the minimum practice consist of five minutes of movement and five minutes of meditation, done at least once a day. Doing ten minutes of each is better.

Try a different combination of exercise and meditation each day, and record your experiences. Once you have experienced each possible combination, choose the one that suits you best. As you continue to practice, you can adapt and change your daily practice to suit your current needs or situation.

Doing a daily energy practice was difficult for me in the beginning. Resistance to change is an important aspect of our makeup and protects us from certain dynamics in our lives. To make changes for healing, it is important to find out where your resistance lies and to find a way around it. My resistance to a daily practice lay in the starting of the practice each day; once I got into it, I loved it.

I worked around my resistance by starting a group that met at my house at 6:00 a.m. I offered morning movement and meditation—no charge, just come and join me. I would wake up at 5:40, sleepily walk downstairs and make morning coffee or tea. I would have the same thought each morning, "This is the last time I will offer this. I hate waking up early. I do not want to do this again. After we meditate, I will announce that this is the last day of the group." Then I would go into the room, start the movement, and within two minutes I would think, "Gosh, I love doing this! I am so glad we are doing this!" Then I would thank the group for coming. Each day went the same, until after six months, when I could do the practice without this incentive.

You may want to start your own group for an extended practice once a week. Group energy often helps us to perform these exercises for longer periods of time. I suggest thirty minutes of movement and twenty-five minutes of meditation for an optimal weekly group practice.

SACRED TOUCH

Being able to shift to the heart center is essential for moving healing with our hands. In fact, if you gain only one practice from this book, it should be the art of shifting to the heart center and using what I call Sacred Touch, a means of moving the energy of the heart center to other parts of our body via our hands.

Sacred Touch is a cornerstone of self-healing with energy medicine. In Sacred Touch, the quality of touch is more important than who is doing the touching. In fact, I am not sure the body cares who is touching it; it cares only about the quality of the touch. Activating the heart center and conferring its energy to the hands allows much communion, communication, and awareness. You can do this very quickly by sending reverence, awe, and compassion from your hands into your body with your touch. The body becomes alive with this touch, and a relationship begins to develop between your hands and the tissue of the body your hands are touching. I begin each Heart Center Meditation with the art of Sacred Touch as it informs and stimulates the body that the meditation has begun. You can practice Sacred Touch all day long.

The Practice

Find a comfortable seated position. Close your eyes. Place your right hand over your heart area, above your sternum, between the breasts.

Place your left hand over your right hand, thumbs touching. (This is the same position we used in the Heart Center Meditation.)

Place your awareness into your hands. Touch your chest as if it were the most sacred object you've ever had the experience of touching. Send compassion, gratitude, and reverence into your body. This is Sacred Touch. Now see if you can pitch your awareness into your body. How is the quality of this touch? How does this touch feel?

Now drop your hands onto your thighs. Send gratitude, compassion, and reverence into your legs. Thank them. Then pitch your awareness into your legs. How does this touch feel? What is the quality of the touch that your hands are placing on your legs?

Now send fear into your legs, in order to feel the difference between Sacred Touch and other types of touch. Touch your own legs as if you were touching something you were afraid of, or as if you might be touching something rotten. Pitch your awareness into your legs now. How does this touch feel?

Move back into Sacred Touch, with compassion, gratitude, and reverence, and see if you can feel a difference. How does Sacred Touch feel now?

Take your hands off your legs, gently shake out your hands, and place them back on your legs casually. How does that touch feel?

Move back to Sacred Touch. Place compassion, gratitude, and reverence into your legs and send them a thank you for this exercise.

When to Use Sacred Touch

Sacred Touch is a simple practice that opens and deepens, meaning that you will learn more and more as you do it, and it will reveal more and more dimensions of itself to you.

Sacred Touch allows you to begin to merge with most energy fields. I suggest that you use Sacred Touch with everything you touch—even with animals, plants, and objects. Everything is sacred, and when we practice Sacred Touch, we experience a body-full awareness of the sacred aspect of life. Use Sacred Touch with all of the other energy healing practices I am sharing with you in this book.

I know that others can tell the difference between casual touch and Sacred Touch. Even if I don't tell them that I'm using Sacred Touch, I can tell from their response that their body knows the quality of the touch that I'm sending. This is clearest with my advanced-dementia patients. People with very advanced dementia no longer communicate with the world around them, and they will sit or lie with their eyes closed all day long. When I examine them with casual or normal touch, they are uncommunicative and keep their eyes closed. When I use Sacred Touch, they often open their eyes and look directly into mine for a moment, before going back "out," closing their eyes and becoming uncommunicative. This is how powerful Sacred Touch is. It communicates at a very deep level—so deep that it can reach someone who is almost impossible to reach.

CHAPTER 5

Sensing and Moving Energy

My body caught fire like an ember
As I brought the syllable OM
The one that says You are That
Into me

—Lalla, *Naked Song*

We are constantly using the entire body as our tool for sensing, feeling, and moving energy, whether or not our minds are aware of it. Our awareness is cueing us all the time, whether we are with another person or with our pets, out in nature, or just thinking of someone. In chapter 4, we practiced the art of Sacred Touch, which allows us to begin to merge with energy fields through touch. In this chapter, we will deepen this work of sensing and moving energy by doing more exercises with our hands and with the breath.

All of these practices are arts; the longer we practice them, the more sensitive we will become to energy and the more information we can glean. Learning to work with energy is like learning a language. At first we can say *yes, no, please,* and *thank you,* and perhaps we can buy necessities at a store. Over time, as we become better at the language, we can use the phone or have conversations in it. Eventually we can even begin to understand another culture through its language.

I sense and learn things through touch that I otherwise would not know or have access to. When I touch someone, details that I was not able to glean through the person's story or symptoms often appear in my awareness. One dramatic example happened many years ago. A woman came to my office with chronic abdominal pain, which came in cycles every six months or so and lasted for a few days. Over twenty years, she had many tests and medical workups for this pain. The tests revealed nothing; all were normal. I listened to her, asked some questions, and then moved her to the table for an examination of her belly.

The moment I put my hand on her, I blurted out, "Oh, you lost a child!" I was surprised to hear myself say it, and I was worried about how she'd respond. She said, "Yes, and I am still upset about it!" She had been pregnant and had lost the child more than thirty years before, and her feelings still had not resolved. It is possible her cycles of abdominal pain were occurring as the stored energy of the experience and of unresolved emotions in her body were activated repeatedly. Most likely her body was trying to express this energy or move it through the energy body for healing. I know it was this energy that was transmitted to me as an image and a knowing, through my hands to my brain and out of my mouth.

As I examined the woman, we discussed this loss. I was moved to tears by her story and the depth of her grief. I kept my hands on her belly during the exam as she told me the details of her loss. I did not say aloud that the pain in her abdomen was connected to the loss of her unborn child, yet I made the connection by being a witness to her experience and by "running" energy. Her pain resolved, and she did not return to the office again. Though I've never learned whether her pain resolved completely or just for that cycle, I still remember how amazed I was to have picked up her story just by touching her. So much is conveyed through touch that it continues to boggle my rational, Western-medical mind.

INITIATING THE HANDS FOR ENERGY WORK

Most healing modalities use a practice to initiate the hands for working with or "running" energy. The initiation is an event or action that opens the hands for healing. Because you may not have been trained in a healing modality, we will start our hands-on healing work with an initiation of your hands. This initiation needs to be done only once, although you may use it in the future to activate your hands before doing healing work on yourself or another. Whether you use it for each session or not, notice that once your hands are initiated in the practice below, they will likely "turn on" naturally when you practice Sacred Touch or move into the energy of the heart center. Begin to pay attention to when your hands are on; noticing how and when they are is valuable to know if you choose to do healing work on other people or animals.

To initiate your hands for healing work, we will use a quick practice that uses sound. Sound moves energy through both tone and vibration. When I begin an energy session, I often will do this next toning exercise, in addition to Sacred Touch, to activate my hands for energy healing.

Before You Start

Sound and vibration can move a tremendous amount of energy. We will initiate our hands for energy healing by applying our voice on our hands. We will use the word *Om* (or *Aum*), a Sanskrit word that means the "manifestation of God in form," or "a reflection of the absolute reality," or "the vibration of the supreme."[1] It's a word with a powerful vibration, so I think Om is a wonderful word for this initiation (see figure 16).

If you are uncomfortable with Om, pick a different meaningful word or tone. It may be a prayerful word, a word from your healing or spiritual tradition, or one of the words from the Heart Center Meditation. Make sure it is a word or tone that has deep meaning for you.

Besides initiating your hands, this exercise will help you become aware of how vibration and energy feel in your hands. Anyone can do this exercise; you may use it anytime you'd like.

The Practice

Sit in a comfortable position and rub your hands together. Stop rubbing and allow yourself to feel any sensations on or in your palms.

Place your left hand close to your mouth and make the sound *Om* (*Aum*—a prolonged tone) three times into the palm. Use a loud voice and see whether you can project your voice *into* your palm.

Then close your eyes and focus your awareness on your palm. What do you notice?

Drop your left hand and pick up your right hand. Do the same thing with the right palm, again, with three tones.

Now notice both hands and your palms. How do they feel?

NOTICING ENERGY BETWEEN THE HANDS

This exercise will allow you to play with energy. Once you become aware of energy, you may be able to feel it, see it, or sense it through a knowing or a vibrational feeling. To me, energy feels like a vibration or density, although we all experience it differently. My clients say that my hands feel hot when I am working on them, although heat is not an accurate way to measure energy. Some healers' hands turn beet red, while others' hands appear to have no changes at all.

Figure 16: The visual image of the Om symbol is just as energetically potent as the Om sound. Viewing it can induct you into the energy of Om and impact the upper dan tien.

The Practice

Sit with your arms at your sides, elbows bent so your hands are in front of you, palms facing each other about three feet apart. Close your eyes and slowly bring your hands toward each other. Notice any sensations that you feel on the way. Notice the layers or any sensation that changes. Very slowly bring your hands all the way together.

Return your hands to their starting position about three feet apart. This time, as you bring your hands in together, see if you notice a layer or a place where you're aware of energy. When you feel it, keep your hands there. Try to make a ball of energy right at the edges of the energy that you feel. Bounce the energy ball slowly back and forth between your hands until you can feel its consistency.

If you don't feel any energy at all, then start over, this time with your hands about eight inches apart. Gently move them back and forth, toward each other and away from each other, and see if you can feel the energy ball. Some people describe the feeling of a rubber band between their hands; others say it feels like having magnets on each hand, which are attracted to and repelled by each other. Stay with this sensation for as long as you'd like. When you've finished, shake out your hands.

CLEARING ENERGY FROM THE HANDS

The hands can become full of energy or full of sensation from time to time. Once you feel energy, you may notice that your ability to sense it shifts: sometimes it's active, sometimes you can no longer sense anything. I call the shift to sensing nothing *being full*. The hands are so full of energy that the sensation begins to dampen. One of my teachers, Brugh Joy—a physician, mystic, and energy healer—explained the shift this way: "Once you are moving at the speed of wind, you no longer feel the wind."

To renew sensation, you need to clear your hands by quickly shaking them out or by giving them quick spritzes of water. Shamans use shaman juice, a concoction of alcohol, witch hazel, and oils or herbs or flowers. You can make a spritzer bottle of alcohol and an essential oil; I like rose, orange, grapefruit, or peppermint. In many stores, you can buy *Agua Florida* (flower water) that also helps with clearing the hands and aura. I keep a spray bottle of my concoction close by and use it on my hands and body between clients or during a session when I feel my hands are sluggish or no longer sensitive.

Expect the sensations to change as you begin to "move at the speed of the wind." I felt a lot more energy twenty years ago, and now I normally feel resistance only where there is a block.

SCANNING THE ENERGY FIELD

Now that your hands are initiated and activated and you've begun to sense energy, we will begin to practice the art of scanning the body's energy field.

Scanning Your Own Energy Field

Sit in a chair in a comfortable position. Raise your right hand, palm down, about three feet above your right thigh. What do you sense? Slowly bring your right palm down toward your leg (figure 17). Notice any sensations that you feel in your hand. What you are feeling is the aura, the layers of your energy body that surrounds your physical body. The aura itself has layers within it. You can feel these layers in the energy field as you bring your hand closer to your leg. They may feel prickly or like heat. I sense them as a density change or an edge as I go through the aura. Most people perceive and describe their sensation a little differently. Notice what you feel instead of trying to conform to what I have described.

Bring your hand all the way down to your right leg. Now raise your hand back to about a foot above your leg. Notice what you feel.

Next, move your hand sideways, quite a distance away from your leg and body, and notice what you feel when it's not above any part of your body. Then bring your hand back over your leg. Quite a bit of the skill in sensing energy is differentiating sensations. Playing with moving your hand over your leg and then away from you leg, over the floor, will help you to start to develop an awareness of your own energy field.

Take a moment and do this same exercise with your left hand and leg. Initially, one hand will be more sensitive to energy than the other.

Again, position your left hand about three feet above your left thigh and slowly lower it. Playing with energy and sensation again, see if you can feel a difference in your hand when it's high above your thigh compared to near your thigh. How does the aura feel close to your leg compared to when your hand is at a distance? Again, try moving your hand laterally off the leg and back over it so you get the sensation of moving out of the leg's aura and then back into it.

Scanning Others' Energy Fields

Normally it's easier to feel the energy field of another person—or the energy field of a pet or plant—than it is to feel our own. So, you may want to try this exercise with another person, to hone your ability to feel energy. Contrast is an important aspect of feeling differences. Starting with our own fields is wonderful and easy, but working on other energy fields and comparing them to our own will help us learn to identify new and unfamiliar sensations. If possible, find someone else or another living thing on which to practicing sensing energy.

Figure 17: To begin scanning your energy field, start with your right hand, palm down, about three feet above your right thigh. Slowly move your hand down toward your leg, feeling the layers of the energy body as you go.

MOVING ENERGY WITH ATTENTION
AND AWARENESS

Energy is moving in the environment and in our bodies all the time. Moving energy in a more purposeful way requires *two points of focus:* attention and awareness.

When I use the word *attention* here, I mean using any of your faculties to bring your focus to the energy in your body. You can do this through the mind by using visualization, images, or words. Or you can operate through the other senses: through the sensation of touch; through hearing, by listening or using the power of word or tone; and even through smell if this is how energy presents itself to you. One of these faculties will bring your attention to your ability to move energy. Next you need to add or connect to awareness.

Awareness is the presence of the unified energy field; it is the presence of that which is all around us. You can make the leap here that awareness is actually external to us, and we are bringing it in. As explained in chapter 2, awareness is the actual substance of the unified field of energy, and the amount of awareness available to us depends on our connection with the larger field.

Awareness is best brought in or accessed by the breath and emotion. However, any second point of attention—sight, hearing, smell—can also bring awareness. While two points of focus are good, three are even better. For example, in the Heart Center Meditation, we use the hands (touch) and silent attributes (the mind), and very often I also use the breath and feeling. This is four points of focus, and it moves a lot of energy to the heart center. Music that you use only for meditation will add a fifth point, music that inducts you.

Do not worry about awareness initially. With time, you will find that the awareness can come in as any second point of attention. The unified or shamanic field of energy comes in as the energy begins to move, because energy is awareness. We usually talk about awareness in a personal way—"my awareness" or "our awareness"—because it is the part of the larger, all-encompassing awareness that is available to each of us in the moment. It is a radical shift when you drop into the concept that it is a field of awareness we are in contact or connection with. The same is true for energy; it is not "ours," yet when we talk about "our energy," it is the energy of the unified or shamanic field we are in touch with or in contact with in the moment. As you work with these concepts, you can add more points of attention and awareness to see how to best move energy in your body.

For these next two practices, we will use breath for awareness and our hands as a focus of attention. (By the way, if you add breath and touch to any guided visualization, the energy that moves in the visualization will be further augmented.) The clearing and grounding techniques you have practiced in chapter 3 have used two points of focus. Toe Tapping uses movement in the hips and legs and the sensation of the tapping in the feet. Add a controlled breath, and Toe Tapping will move more energy. The same is true with Shaking the Bones: we use movement, and the breath naturally moves with this exercise. We can also add rhythm of sound to move more energy. Again, if you're confused, don't worry. Energy movement happens naturally as your body and the energy body find ways to add a second and even a third point of attention or awareness.

We will also begin to practice using multiple points of focus in the next exercises. To experience the use of attention and awareness for moving energy, we will start with two simple breathing techniques: the Abdominal Breath and the Root Chakra Breath. Both of these breathing techniques can move energy immediately within the body.

THE ABDOMINAL BREATH

When the energy in our energy body is out of balance, such as when there is too much energy in the head (the most common energy imbalance in our culture), the autonomic or sympathetic nervous system is affected; that's the part of us responsible for the fight-or-flight response, relaxation, heart rate, and even blood pressure. When we're in an unbalanced state, our nervous system can end up with too much of the sympathetic nervous system turned on, putting us in a constant, mild, fight-or-flight state.

This Abdominal Breath, also called the diaphragmatic breath, has an immediate effect on the physical body as well as the energy body. It shifts the balance of energy into the lower abdominal area, increasing the parasympathetic tone (relaxation) and decreasing the sympathetic tone (the fight-or-flight response). The nervous system will naturally do something to bring itself back to homeostasis or balance whenever it begins to move out of balance. About a month after I'd started practicing this Abdominal Breath, I noticed that I would move into abdominal breathing without even thinking about it. When I paid close attention to what was happening, I noticed that the moment something was about to set me off, my body, ready to return to homeostasis, would start abdominal breathing. My nervous system would stay settled, and my energy body would stay rooted in the physical body instead of becoming unbalanced. That is what we want to happen—we want to practice a breath exercise often enough that the body begins to shift into it naturally and without effort when the nervous system and energy body need to maintain its balance or be rebalanced.

Before You Start

Set a timer for this exercise so that you are not distracted by the need to keep track of time. I suggest you do the exercise for five minutes at a time until you become used to it.

The Practice

Sit in a comfortable position. Place your hands, one on top of the other, over your lower abdomen, below the belly button and above the pubic bone (figure 18). Close your eyes and breathe into your hands. As you breathe, the lower abdomen will inflate with the inhale and deflate on the exhale. If breathing into your hands seems difficult, use the visualization of filling a balloon in your lower abdomen,.

If you are still having difficulty, try this breath lying flat on your back. The diaphragm has an easier time in a flat position, as it is pushed down in this technique to bring the breath in. (Normal breathing uses the chest muscles to bring in the breath.) This is why the lower abdomen extends out on the inhale and retracts on the exhale.

It takes ten or fifteen breaths to begin to do this type of breathing properly. Continue breathing at your own pace, focusing all your awareness and attention on your lower abdomen as you do.

At the end of five minutes, remove your hands. Come back to the room, open your eyes, and notice how you feel.

When to Use the Abdominal Breath

Once you become adept at the Abdominal Breath, you can practice it with your eyes open. At some point, practice without your hands and use your mind and sensation of the breath and energy as the points of attention and awareness. Being able to do this practice without your hands on your abdomen will enable you to use the Abdominal Breath while you are out in the world. Try using this practice for two minutes at a time, multiple times a day. When I first practiced this breath, I did it as many times as I could throughout the day, whenever I remembered to engage it.

Figure 18: For the Abdominal Breath, place your hands, one on top of the other, over your lower abdomen. Breathe into your hands, inflating the abdomen on the inhale and deflating it on the exhale.

If you want to see the Abdominal Breath in action, watch a baby. Most infants naturally use the Abdominal Breath for the first six to nine months. Also, watch people who are in a very relaxed state or sleeping; they often shift to the Abdominal Breath as soon as they begin to sleep. In my healing work, clients normally shift naturally to the Abdominal Breath when they are lying on their back and are relaxed. You can also notice your breath while you are having a massage; if it is not a painful massage, you'll find that your body does this breathing pattern naturally.

THE ROOT CHAKRA BREATH

The Root Chakra Breath is more grounding than the Abdominal Breath. It uses attention and awareness to connect you to the energy field through the root chakra. We call this being connected to the energy field of the earth.

Before You Start

As with the Abdominal Breath, set a timer for this exercise so you are not distracted by having to keep track of time. Again, I suggest you practice this for five minutes the first time.

The Practice

Sit comfortably and place your hands on your root chakra area—the perineal area between your legs (figure 19). Close your eyes and bring your attention to your hands on the perineal area. Now add awareness, through the breath, to your root chakra with each inhale. On the exhale, follow your breath back up and out through your mouth. You can do this in one breath now: inhale and bring your breath in your mouth or nose, down the wind pipe, through the torso down to the root chakra and to your hands. Exhale as you follow your breath back up and out through the mouth. Once you are able to do this, then it is more simple: inhale into the root chakra and exhale through the mouth.

Breathe at your own pace for five minutes.

Once you have become adept at the Root Chakra Breath, try it with your eyes open. Try practicing without your hands, using your mind for attention and pitching your mind to the sensation in your root chakra. Keep using the breath as the point of awareness or second point of focus. Once you are adept at this breath with your eyes open and without your hands, you can use it at work, in the line at the grocery store, or at any point during the day. If you are using this breath in a private place, keep your hands on the perineal area to augment the attention aspect of moving energy.

After the Root Chakra Breath becomes easy, see if you can focus your breath beyond your root chakra—in the earth. This extended focus may take some practice. Mastery of this entails visualizing each breath going to the root chakra and then down into the core of the earth. You can do this with your mouth open or closed. The breath travels down the windpipe, continues into the root chakra, and then travels down into the earth. On each exhale, follow the breath back out the mouth. I use my hands during this breath.

Figure 19: For the Root Chakra Breath, place your hands over the perineal area. See your breath traveling into your mouth and nose and down through your body to the root chakra and your hands. Then see it traveling back up the body and out.

When to Use the Root Chakra Breath

Use this breath whenever you feel the need to be grounded, such as when you've been startled, are thinking too much, or are having an "off" day. Try using it for two minutes at a time, multiple times during the day, and see how your day changes.

You may want to connect this Root Chakra Breath or the Abdominal Breath to an activity so that you remember to do it often. For example, you could practice the Abdominal Breath every time you look at a clock, or you could use the Root Chakra Breath each time you sit down. I like to connect the Root Chakra Breath to activities done in a seated position, especially those for which I am seated on the floor or outside on the earth.

THE CIRCULAR BREATH

This exercise, the Circular Breath, will help you begin to notice the circular flow of energy within the body and recognize gates in the energy body. Gates are places in the energy flow where energy can be concentrated, blocked, or drain energy out of our personal field, like a leak. This Circular Breath works with the energy gate at the back of the neck, right under the occiput (the back of the skull), another at the sacrum, and a third at the navel. These three areas are often the locations of energy leaks or blocks. They can connect us to the larger energy field around us, yet it is better if these gates are closed. If these gates are open or draining energy all the time, we can have problems with fatigue. We can get "hooked" at these points in our body by the energy of a larger group, such as our family or clan, and even the collective unconscious. Some healers will go as far as cutting "cords" at these sites. I find it easier and more effective to use this Circular Breath to allow the body to heal these sites itself.

Before You Start

Set a timer for five minutes. As with the other breathing techniques, once you get the hang of this exercise, you can use it for shorter periods of time. Take a good look at the diagram of this breath (figure 20); it will help you understand the description below.

The Practice

Sit in a comfortable position and close your eyes. Place your hands on your lower abdomen or lower dan tien. Inhale, and as you do, imagine pulling the breath downward, from your lower abdomen through the perineal area between your legs to your sacrum. Then visualize the breath moving up your spine to the back of your skull, up over the top of your head, and to your forehead. Then, on the exhale, see the breath/energy and the awareness from the forehead moving back down the front of your body to your lower abdomen.

Visualizing the entire circular pathway takes time to learn, and you might not get it on the first breath. Just keep doing the breath until you can visualize the energy moving all the way around the body with one breath. Notice places where you have difficulty. These places are likely areas that need some work (such as places where a leak needs to be sealed), and this breath helps with that. You may notice that the sacrum and back of the head are places where you

Figure 20: With the Circular Breath, use your awareness to see the breath traveling through the body in the pattern shown.

can get stuck. You can also tap on these areas to clear the flow; then go back and try the Circular Breath again.

When to Use the Circular Breath

Use this breath whenever you need deep relaxation. It's wonderful for pain relief any time you are having a painful procedure or body work or if you need to lie still when you're experiencing discomfort. It's also very useful when you're feeling chaotic, stressed, defensive, or agitated. The sacrum is a very important center because it enables us to stand on our own without losing our center when life sends a wobble that we didn't expect. I suggest that you learn this breathing technique very well and that you practice it two or three times a day for at least two minutes each time until it is effortless. After that, you can call upon this exercise when you need it, and you'll know as soon as you start getting off balance that it's time to bring in the Circular Breath.

THE FULL-BODY ENERGY CONNECTION

Next we will practice one of the cornerstones of healing, the Full-Body Energy Connection. I learned this practice from Dr. Brugh Joy, yet many popular energy-healing modalities have a full-body connection similar to this one.[2]

The Full-Body Energy Connection balances the entire energy body and will also do specific repair work. This practice is the crux of energy self-healing; when you see energy healers, this practice is the kind of work they primarily focus on. If you do the clearing and opening movement exercises from chapter 3 daily, this balancing and repair work will be easier. I recommend you do this body-balancing exercise weekly. It is useful even if you do get frequent sessions with an energy healer.

Before You Start

Anyone can do this exercise. You will need a clock and a place where you can sit comfortably with your legs extended (the floor, your bed, or a couch). Have the diagrams (figures 21a through 21n) next to you so that you can see how to place your hands.

The Practice

Sit in a comfortable position with your legs extended. Turn your left leg out and bend that knee to bring your left foot up to your inner right thigh (figure 21a). Place your right hand on your left foot and place your left hand on your left knee. Connect to your lower leg using Sacred Touch with both hands. Feel a connection between the hands and through the leg.

Using Sacred Touch, send energy from the right hand to the left hand. Then send energy from the left hand back to the right hand. Flood the lower leg with energy. Pour in compassion, gratitude, and reverence.

Now straighten your left leg, extending it next to your right. Move the right hand to the left knee and the left hand to the left hip (figure 21b). Connect to your upper leg with both hands, using Sacred Touch. Feel a connection between the hands through the leg. Using Sacred Touch, send energy from the right hand to the left hand. Then send energy from the left hand back to the right hand. Flood the upper leg with energy. Pour in compassion, gratitude, and reverence.

Switch to the other leg. Bend your right leg to bring your right foot up to your inner left thigh. Place your left hand on your right foot and your right hand on your right knee. Connect to your leg using Sacred Touch with both hands. Feel a connection between the hands through the leg. Using Sacred Touch, send energy from the right hand to the left hand, and then send energy from the left hand back to the right hand. Flood the lower leg with energy. Pour in compassion, gratitude, and reverence.

Continue in this same pattern to connect the rest of the body. Remember to connect both hands through the body and, with Sacred Touch, flood each area with compassion, gratitude, and reverence. Spend at least one minute in each area after you feel a connection. Continue in this order:

- Left hand to your right knee and your right hand to your right hip

- Left hand on your left hip and your right hand on your right hip (figure 21c)

- Right hand between your legs and your left hand over your lower abdomen, below the navel and above the pubic bone (figure 21d)

- Right hand over your solar plexus area below the ribs and your left hand over your lower abdomen (figure 21e)

- Left hand to your heart and your right hand over your solar plexus area (figure 21f)

- Both hands over the heart area: place your left hand on top of your right hand, thumbs touching (figure 21g)

- Right hand on your left shoulder and your left hand on your heart (figure 21h)

- Left hand on your right shoulder and your right hand over your heart (figure 21i)

- Right hand on your heart and your left hand on your throat area (figure 21j)

- Right hand on your forehead and your left hand on the throat (figure 21k)

- Right hand on your forehead and your left hand on the crown of your head (figure 21l)

- Both hands on top of your head, with your left hand on the left side and your right hand on the right side (figure 21m)

- Left hand on top of your head and your right hand about a foot above your head, with the palm upward toward the sky (figure 21n)

To end this practice, lie flat on your back with your arms at your sides. Relax in this position and receive the healing work you did on yourself. Notice how you feel, assessing how your body has responded. Stay relaxed for three to five minutes. You may then get up and move to the next activity in your day.

FULL-BODY ENERGY CONNECTION

Figure 21a: First position—
right hand on left foot, left hand
on left knee

Figure 21b: Second position—
right hand on left knee, left hand
on left hip

Figure 21c: Third position—
right hand on right hip, left hand
on left hip

Figure 21d: Fourth position—
right hand on perineal area, between
the legs; left hand on abdomen

Figure 21e: Fifth position—right hand on solar plexus, left hand on abdomen

Figure 21f: Sixth position—right hand on solar plexus, left hand on heart

Figure 21g: Seventh position—left hand over the heart, right hand over the left, thumbs touching

Figure 21h: Eighth position—right hand on left shoulder, left hand over the heart

Figure 21i: Ninth position—right hand on the heart, left hand on the right shoulder

Figure 21j: Tenth position—right hand on the heart, left hand on the throat

Figure 21k: Eleventh position—right hand on the forehead, left hand on the throat

Figure 21l: Twelfth position—right hand on forehead, left hand on the crown of the head

Figure 21m: Thirteenth position—right hand on the right side of the head, left hand on the left side of the head

Figure 21n: Last position—right hand above the head, palm facing upward; left hand on the crown of the head

When to Use the Full-Body Energy Connection

This is a wonderful weekly exercise. You can do the full-length practice even if you have chronic pain; it's so gentle, you can do it without side effects. This practice is also the basis of practicing healing on others, if you are so inclined.

USING TOOLS TO MOVE ENERGY

We have already discussed using a handheld vibrating massager to move energy in your back or other places you cannot reach. You may also use the massager wherever you have a block or you notice pain. As we discussed in chapter 1, the site of the energy block may not be right at the area of the pain, so remember to work around the area, especially on areas closer to the center of your body. If you have areas that are more sensitive to body tapping, those are also good places to use the massager.

Rattles can be used to move a tremendous amount of energy. Rattles break up stagnant energy, tangles, or blocks. Try making a rattle[3] or buying a rattle (at a music store), then shake it over parts of your body where you have any form of difficulty, such as pain, stagnant energy, or low energy flow. You are shaking it in your aura; because the energy in the aura is connected to the energy inside the body, the sound and vibration will have an impact there. Remember, if the problem is in an extremity, the block is often upstream from the problem. For example, with foot pain, rattle over your knee and hip as well as the foot because the block can be in any or all three of these sites.

Tuning forks and bowls also move energy with their vibration and sound. Touching the single end of the tuning fork to specific places can have a wonderful impact on the energy body. Experience is the best way to assess the effects of a tuning fork. Try it to see how it feels and what you notice. Touch the end of the tuning fork to any part of your body. You can use it on a tight jaw, over a tendon that is bothering you, on your forehead, or on your heart chakra to open these areas more.

Toning bowls are also lovely tools to move energy. The best way to use a toning bowl is to place a fabric cover, towel, or blanket on your body, place the bowl on top of the blanket, and play the bowl while it sits on you. This is best done on your torso. If you use two bowls, notice when they entrain and how the energy in your body moves from one bowl to the other. I like to place one bowl on the lower dan tien, one over the heart, and one on the forehead. Play all three and notice the infusion throughout your body. Be careful if you have chronic pain in your abdomen because increased energy in your abdomen may increase the pain. With chronic pain, start by playing the bowl(s) for a very short period of time.

Feathers are wonderful tools to use in the aura. Combing a feather smoothes out or brings into harmony the energy it touches. I often will use a feather after a rattle; the rattle will shake up a block or tangle, and the feather will smooth the energy back to its original pattern or untangled state. I finish many healing sessions on my clients by using a feather in the aura, about a foot off the body. A feather is wonderful for clearing energy out of the aura, too. You may use large feathers, such as a peacock or ostrich, or smaller feathers such as a crow or turkey vulture.

Many cultures use smoke in the form of incense or a smudge stick made of herbs like sage or copal (a resin) to clear energy. To smudge the body, light some sage or incense and sweep the smoke around the body to cleanse the aura. You can also smudge a room to clear out old or stagnant energy.

CHAPTER 6

Balance, Alignment, and Body Wisdom

*Your thoughts are like a child fretting
near its mother's breast, restless
and afraid, who with a little guidance
can find the path of courage*

—Lalla, *Naked Song*

Balance is normally defined as "harmonious or proper arrange-ment"[1] or "mental and emotional steadiness."[2] Regarding the energy body and health, balance rests on two important aspects: the distribution of energy between the upper body, heart, and lower body, and a good flow of energy throughout the body. When explor-ing and working with balance, I prefer to start with the paradigm of the dan tiens from traditional Chinese medicine. There needs to be a balance of energy between the lower dan tien or primary energy center, the middle dan tien or heart area, and upper dan tien or head area. The rule of balance among these three is *cool head, neutral heart,* and *warm pelvis.*[3] This means that the majority of the energy in the body ought to be centered in the lower dan tien or lower abdominal area. The heart is the midpoint, and optimally there is less energy in the head (figure 22).

In our culture, I commonly see that people are flipped in this balance, with a warm head, neutral heart, and cool pelvis. The bulk of the energy in the body is carried too high. This makes it hard to allow the energy of emotions and experiences to flow naturally through the energy body into resolution. Chapter 3 discussed how people often pull energy to the head too quickly instead of allowing it to flow naturally through their entire body and energy body. When a vibration or experience that is considered unpleasant comes in, bringing the energy down into the lower dan tien or lower chakras will naturally prevent an ungrounded, or asustado, response. When the energy of emotion or experience does not flow through the body, it can create an energy tag in the energy body, which then needs to be cleared or we tend to relive what has happened. The energy in the body will reactivate this tag over and over. (If you have ever had a feeling reactivate or memory pop up during a massage, this was what was happening—an energy tag was being activated.)

Figure 22: The ideal balance of energy in the body: Most of the body's energy is centered in the lower dan tien (the abdomen). There is less energy in the middle dan tien (the heart), and even less in the upper dan tien (the head).

I want to differentiate between feeling and emotion. Emotion is *energy* in motion; feeling is this energy at the level of the third chakra. We identify this energy as feeling when it is processed through the third chakra. It is wonderful to experience feelings. If we take emotion as it is, as energy in motion, then grief, sadness, difficulty, and even wonderful and joyful feelings (we get as attached to joyful feelings as we do to difficult feelings) can be brought down to the root and second chakra or lower dan tien. Moving emotions down will ground the energy in the body and transform the feeling (third-chakra activity) into energy at the lower dan tien or the root and second chakras. Once grounded and transformed at the level of energy, the energy naturally travels back up through the chakras and dan tiens. As it does, the energy often sparks creativity or action. In fact, the energy of the emotion or experience will create more energy or vitality for the entire energy system in the body.

Moving the energy of emotions or experiences down to the lower energy centers is the second most important teaching in this book, second only to the activating and using energy of the heart center. In this chapter, I will teach you the beginning steps to moving the energy of emotion and experience into the lower dan tien or root and second chakras. Doing so might be awkward at first, because of the perspective of our rational culture and how we've been socialized. (Want to see how often our culture encourages us to cut off energy to our lower centers? Just watch how many people cross their legs.) But bringing down the energy again and again balances energy in the body as well as vitality at the level of the lower dan tien. Bringing down the energy of any emotion or experience—even through the legs (use Toe Tapping while you bring it down)—actually clears the channels of energy. Then the energy will naturally move back up through the body and recirculate as energy. You will have to practice this energy movement over and over until it becomes second nature. Because it takes two points of focus to move energy, focusing attention on where energy in the body is active and using simple movement or breath techniques to shift the location and movement of energy is the beginning of assisting the movement of energy into proper alignment.

Balance also refers to the balance of the autonomic nervous system—the balance between the sympathetic (fight-or-flight) response and the parasympathetic (relaxation) response. The sympathetic response is our stress response; it causes our peripheral circulation to shut down, sends more blood to the internal organs, increases our heart rate, and increases our blood pressure. This response should be in balance with the parasympathetic relaxation response, which allows blood to flow to the extremities, decreases the heart rate, and lowers the blood pressure as we relax. A healthy nervous system can move from a sympathetic state of stress to a balance of the sympathetic and parasympathetic quickly. So maintaining balance in the autonomic nervous system means maintaining the ability to move back to homeostasis quickly at the level of the nervous system, as we discussed in chapter 3.

Many years ago, I received a lesson in the importance of energy balance when I shaved my head. I had heard a story of the Indian saint Babaji, who described mundan, head shaving, thus: "Just think of the top of your head as a helipad, and shaving it makes it easier for me land." This, to me, meant that shaving my head would open my crown chakra. So I went ahead, after the nausea of letting go of my hair and appearance. I found that, within a day, the energy body shifted into its ideal balance: cool head, neutral heart, and warm pelvis. I kept shaving my head until I could reach this alignment through energy practices. Even my kids noticed a difference. "Mommy is much nicer with her head shaved," said my six-year-old daughter. Her comment was the best evidence that I was not "hot headed" anymore. I kept my hair shaved or very short for the next two years, until I felt I could keep my energy balanced without the head shaving.

I'm not suggesting that you shave your head, but I think this chapter's explorations of awareness and balance will help you discern how you carry energy in your body. Once you can make this discernment, you can begin to practice the art of moving energy in your body in order to access more vitality and so that energy can clear and recirculate the way it did when you were born.

Balance in the energy body means that there is a good flow of energy throughout the body and that the energy body is in a constant state of flow or movement. What many healers call "balancing the chakras," I think of as grounding the body, clearing the body, and stimulating flow through the body. If you have an area that has consistently low flow, like my lower dan tien when I had my chronic illness, then you have to continue the techniques in the book to bring the energy body into balance (good healthy flow) and alignment. By *alignment*, I mean the healthy flow of energy that aligns itself naturally. If we go back to emotion, an aligned body will take a feeling and root it into the lower energy centers as energy, or e-motion, and then the energy will move back up through the body naturally. In the story I told of my infant daughter in chapter 1, the mudra and the breath she did are indications of a naturally aligned energy system. The energy moved through her energy body naturally, directing itself through her body with the breath and hand movement.

I want to stress that the body and energy body is a living system. If we go back to the analogy of a river with tributaries, it is easy to see that the chakras, dan tiens, matrix, meridians, and aura are in a constant state of flow to greet what the body is doing at the moment. There is not a "proper" or right amount of energy in one place at one time. Balance and alignment are about energy flowing through all the channels without stagnation or overflow. The Full-Body Energy Connection exercise from the last chapter is a wonderful way to work with your entire body to stimulate balance, alignment, and energy flow throughout it. Once the body is grounded and clear and the energy is flowing, the energy goes where it needs to, when it needs to.

You can visit an energy healer if you want feedback about how your energy body is doing, as long as you remember that the healer is getting only a snapshot of you in that moment, not a total picture of your energy flow. For example, if a healer tells you one of your chakras is closed, it is closed in that moment and is probably a pattern for you to work with. However, the chakras open and close all the time, and one reading is just that. Use it to work with, and then reassess your energy body.

PRIMARY AWARENESS EXERCISE

When you get started with energy healing work, you normally carry one state of consciousness at a time. I call this state your *primary awareness*. (This is different from *primal awareness*, a term used to talk about awareness connected to the energy field from the lower chakras.) Your primary awareness is the place where the majority of your energy is focused in your body; it is the awareness most available to you in the current moment.

This exercise will show you where your primary awareness currently is, which is important as you begin to learn to read reality at the level of energy. You need to read what is available in the moment before you are able to carry more than one state of consciousness or awareness. This self-healing work teaches you how to read the energy in your body in order to be able to access and move energy in a purposeful way. When our primary awareness is located in only one place, we are most likely to be heavily involved in an activity that requires this single awareness, like writing (head) or dancing (lower dan tien). The problem is, many of us live our entire lives through only one awareness or state of consciousness. Over time, living this way affects the balance in our energy body and physical body, which in turn affects our health and healing.

For balance and healing, carrying two states of consciousness or carrying two points of awareness, such as the way we used our hands with our breath in the previous chapter, will allow the body to move energy quickly and effectively. Once you get the hang of this, you can move into three states of consciousness or points of awareness. Reality, as noted earlier, is constellated from energy in the body, so we want to learn to use more than one assemblage point in the body. Learning to do so is an important key to learning to read energy and how it is active in your body from moment to moment.

The Practice

Lie flat and close your eyes. Check in with your body. Where is the first place that your attention goes when you check in? Don't think about this—just notice where your attention goes. This is where your primary awareness is at the moment. Is it behind your eyes, in your chest, in your belly, in your legs, in your feet? For most people, it's behind their eyes or in their head. Notice that there is one spot that predominates. Do not change it—just notice it.

Though your energy and awareness is most often in one area of the body more than in than the rest, your primary awareness is not a fixed state or place. Check in frequently during your day to see where your primary awareness is and whether it has shifted. Stop and do this exercise again now before continuing with the next practice.

CARRYING MULTIPLE STATES OF AWARENESS

We are used to carrying or being present to one state of consciousness or one state of awareness at a time. However, it is possible with practice to carry up to four or five. With this exercise, we will begin to explore the possibility that we can carry two states of awareness at once. The goal is to be able to carry more than one state of awareness throughout the day.

The Practice

Lie flat, close your eyes, and scan your body again to find your primary awareness. It may change as you move into relaxation.

Now, place your hands on your lower dan tien, which is your lower abdominal area between your pubic bone and your navel (figure 23). Breathe into your lower dan tien and, using Sacred Touch, flood the area with gratitude and compassion. Try to chord or connect your place of primary awareness with the awareness of your lower dan tien. See if you can keep your attention on your belly and on your place of primary awareness at the same time.

Tap your toes together a few times and rest your hands on your thighs. Now move your hands to your forehead (figure 24). See if you can hold two states of awareness, your toes and your head, at the same time.

Next, place your hands back on your lower dan tien and see if you can hold two states of awareness, your lower dan tien and your head, at the same time.

Figure 23: Place your hands over your lower dan tien. See if you can hold your awareness of both this spot and your primary awareness spot simultaneously.

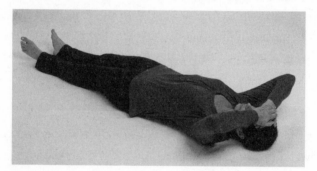

Figure 24: Continue by placing both hands on your forehead. See if you can hold your awareness of this spot, your lower dan tien, and your feet simultaneously.

Figure 25: Finish by placing your hands over your heart (your middle dan tien). See if you can hold your awareness here, your lower dan tien, and your head simultaneously.

Tap your toes together a few times again. See if you can become aware of your feet, your lower dan tien, and your head—all three areas—equally at once. This may be getting difficult, but give it a try. Practice will make this ability more available to you.

Now, leave one hand on your lower dan tien and place the other on your heart, your middle dan tien. See if you can become aware of your lower dan tien, your heart, and your head at the same time. See if you can feel the energy moving back and forth between these two energy centers.

Next, move both hands to the heart center and discern if you can stay in touch with the awareness at the lower dan tien and upper dan tien as you do (figure 25).

When to Carry Multiple States of Awareness

What if you always checked in with your abdomen (lower dan tien), your heart (middle dan tien, the heart center), and your head (upper dan tien)—all three areas—before you made a decision or acted on an idea? These three centers have different wisdoms and experiences of life, and normally we use only our head and upper dan tien to make decisions. I suggest you practice this exercise as often as you can until you become adept at it. Once you are able to carry all three states of awareness, practice checking in with these three centers throughout your day.

I almost always follow the process that enlivens the body, the lower dan tien, not the head or upper dan tien. This is a radical concept for some people. Following the wisdom of the body can be difficult if your life is very structured by a job or activities that the body energy is not in accord with. You may want to start following the vitality of the body on weekends or free days at first. Over time, it gets easier.

If there's conflict between the head and the body, and if I cannot move toward the body alone, I move to the heart, the middle dan tien, before I choose a course of action. The reverence or awe from the heart always affords another perspective and often another solution, or it will allow the upper dan tien and lower dan tien to come into alignment.

AWAKENING THE BODY RESPONSE

Once I got the hang of checking the different centers, I began to use them to check which of my activities—and even people I considered friends—were enlivening to my body. This next exercise, Awakening the Body Response, will help you explore what I'm talking about.

In this exercise, we will check in with the upper and lower dan tiens to see how they respond to activities, people, and problems in your life. Practicing this exercise will teach you to move toward activities that are in the flow of healing instead of trying to force the energy in your body to fit into the way you're living. The key teaching, again, is "cool head, neutral heart, warm pelvis (lower dan tien)." We want to begin to read what helps our lower dan tien move toward vitality, while keeping our heart center open and our upper dan tien cool—functioning, yet quiet from chaotic chatter or monkey mind. I want to reiterate that the mind is a reflection of the body, so a chaotic mind is often a sign that our energy flow is not balanced in the body.

The Practice

Lie on your back in a comfortable position, and close your eyes. Rest your hands on your lower dan tien. Practice the art of Sacred Touch and flood the area with compassion and reverence.

Next, move your hands to your middle dan tien, or heart area, and flood this area with Sacred Touch. Move your hands on your forehead, or upper dan tien, and again flood the area with Sacred Touch. Then rest your hands at your side. Connect to all three centers again.

Using an image and any sensation or emotion that you can, bring into your awareness some activity that you love to do. Place your hands on your lower dan tien. Check in to see if this activity enlivens or quiets your lower dan tien. If this dan tien had an on-off switch, would this activity turn your dan tien on or off? If this part of your body could speak, would it say yes or no? Would it be drawn toward the activity or repelled by the activity?

Drop any expectations here. If you bump into thoughts or reasoning here, you're thinking instead of checking in with the lower dan tien. Try again. Some people need time to learn to check in with the body.

Now move to the upper dan tien, or forehead, and check in. What do you think of this activity that you love? Like it or not like it? On or off? Is this part of your body saying yes or no?

Drop your hand to the side and allow yourself to clear that image.

Continue by using images, feelings, and sensations to bring into your awareness somebody you love to be around, as if he or she were sitting next to you. Place your hands on your lower dan tien and check in. Does this person enliven or quiet it? Does this person enliven your lower dan tien or dampen it? On or off? If this part of your body could speak, would it say yes or no? Is the body drawn toward this person or repelled by him or her? Again, if you bump into thoughts or reasoning, you're thinking instead of checking in with the dan tien. If that happens, try again.

Now, move to the upper dan tien, or forehead, and check in. What do you think of this person who you love to be around? Like or not like? Yes or no?

Drop your hands to your side and clear the person that you love from your awareness.

Now, bring somebody else into your awareness—someone you do not like being around. Use images, feelings, and sensations to bring that person into your awareness. Place your hands on your lower dan tien to see if this person enlivens or quiets this energy center. On or off? Yes or no? Again, if you bump into thoughts or reasoning here, try again.

Move to the upper dan tien. What do you think of this person who you don't like being around? Is the response a yes or no? Is your mind on or off?

Now, take your hands and place them over your heart. How do you experience this person from the level of your heart, from reverence and awe?

Drop your hands back to your side and clear this person from your awareness.

Finally, bring up in your awareness, with image and sensation, a conflict or a problem that you are experiencing in your life.

Place your hands on your lower dan tien. Check in to see if this problem or conflict enlivens or quiets your dan tien. On or off? Yes or no? Does it enliven you or dampen your lower dan tien?

Now move your hands to the upper dan tien and forehead. On or off? Yes or no?

Now move your hands to the heart and middle dan tien and view this conflict from the place of reverence for what is.

Drop your hands to your side and take a few deep breaths.

When to Use Awakening the Body Response

As I discussed before, there are multiple centers of energy in the body and, therefore, multiple choices of how we can experience anything. Together the energy centers form a ladder, and from each rung, we get a different view of the world. Our primary awareness is the rung we stand on most often. How we move to the other rungs and begin to perceive more than just our normal awareness is the art of allowing different experiences of life and healing. Because the chakra system has seven different centers, it's complex for normal, daily, ordinary awareness, which is why I like the dan tiens. I think it's a good goal to have two dan tiens in our awareness as often as possible and to be checking in with all three as often as we can.

The Hopi tradition and TCM see the different organs being different states of consciousness or awareness. Illness, in those modalities, can occur from a conflict between organs. In the Hawaiian healing tradition of Ho'oponopono, illness in the body is seen as stemming from conflict with the family. Experiencing different realities or energies within the body (including the mind, as it is part of the body) is the first step into exploring conflict housed in the body. It can lead you into more healing potential and more vitality. Further, if we understand that illness in the body is the resolution of these conflicts, then sometimes bringing in all the awareness we can about the conflict or different energies from the different parts of the body can lead to a spontaneous resolution or healing of the illness or disease. Transforming illness and disease from the level of consciousness or energy alone is very deep work, not addressed in the scope of this book. While I am giving a brief map here, most of us need to pair energy healing with conventional medicine, TCM, and other healing modalities to engage and heal from disease once it is present in the body.

To further illustrate what I am addressing here, I want to use the concept of a talking circle. In some Native American traditions when a conflict arises in a community, the community comes together and forms a circle. A talking stick is passed around, and each person speaks his or her truth. This continues until the conflict spontaneously resolves. From each person offering his or her perspective and listening to the perspectives of others, a resolution comes out of the circle. Sometimes all the members are satisfied, and sometimes members choose to put their point of view aside for the good of the entire community. The community is balanced and aligned through the process.

The body is like a community of energies and organs. We are learning to hear and feel all the different awarenesses and allow them to dialogue through energy practices until any conflict resolves or until we, through our personal process, can hold the conflict with awareness. I use this talking-circle method with medical students and residents when we plan ceremonies. It is incredible to observe how this nonrational way of planning and weaving different ideas together always brings something forward that is more resourceful and powerful than what voting or making unilateral decisions could have. The same holds true for the body. If we work at the level of energy, harmony occurs in ways we cannot initially imagine.

When I first started checking in with multiple states of awareness, I found that certain things that I thought I didn't like doing actually enlivened the body. In addition, I found that some of my friendships were at the level of the head only and that my body didn't feel particularly alive when I was with these people. Conversely, I found that my head had issues with certain people in my life while my body was very enlivened by them. Paying attention to these kinds of differences is the beginning of paying attention to what is happening at the level of the subtle body, instead of trying to make the energy body fit into how we want our life to go. It's also the beginning of bringing problems to the heart and viewing them with reverence, instead of seeing them only through the head.

Let me tell you one of my favorite stories about this kind of checking in. Once I was on the phone with someone I know. He was complaining quite a bit, first about almost everyone he knew and then about much of the world. Instead of listening to the particular details discussed, I asked myself, "How is my body reacting to this conversation?" I began to notice there was a warm, glowing feeling in my belly and my heart. In fact, the tone of his voice was bathing me in a feeling of healing, and my body was enlivened by his voice and our communication. So I ignored what he was talking about and pitched my awareness to the vibration of his voice. I sat back, closed my eyes, and listened intently to his voice, amazed that I was receiving this wonderful transmission of energy, tucked into this funny rant.

Try out this exercise from time to time. Check in with the body to see if you can perceive what is happening beyond your head. It's my belief that we are privy to little of what's going on energetically between two people or in a crowd, yet with some practice, we can become much more aware of what's happening.

Remember that most people initially have difficulty checking in with the lower dan tien. If you do, go back and use the Toe Tapping exercise (chapter 3) daily. You will feel a difference when you're grounded, when the energy body fully engages the larger energy field of the earth at the root chakra.

ENERGY MOVEMENT AND THE CHAKRAS

In the last exercises, we used the dan tiens system to explore energy in the body. Now I want to go in more deeply with the chakra system. Each chakra interprets energy in a specific, unique way. Exploring the chakras will help you learn to discern the subtle differences in their qualities of energy. Each of the chakras, like the dan tiens, has a different purpose and flow. I have seen multiple charts that tell what each chakra deals with, and I want to caution you not to interpret other people's definitions of the chakras too literally. You need to go into each chakra and find out for yourself what its purpose is.

For example, the root chakra is often described as dealing with survival and money issues. That is not my experience of the root chakra; it is too small a definition, plus "issues" are an incomplete translation of energy. For example, the source of money issues can be the root chakra, second chakra, or third chakra, or they can have something to do with health or parental issues. In fact, what many of us call "money issues" is just a personal preference for how much cash we want. There is also a difference between too much money and not enough money, and each of these two issues may be housed in different portions of the body. *It is energy, not issues, that we want to read.*

I like to look at the chakras according to movement. The root chakra is the lower gate of the energy field. It is the first place vibration can come into the body. When an event occurs, it enters the body as a vibration at the root chakra. From there, it moves to the second chakra, where it begins to become alive or active in the body. This is the start of the creative process, and it's the beginning of our awareness that something has occurred. This is the level where we experience the energy as an instinct or event.

From the second chakra, the energy moves to the third chakra, where it begins to differentiate into more specific processes involved in action, based on the individual body. It is where the energy differentiates into who and what we are, through ego, personal preference, personal love for those in our lives, and it stimulates actions that allow us to live, take care of ourselves, and move through the world as separate individuals. Here, the differentiation of energy allows us to formulate an individual response to the vibrational event.

From the third chakra, if it can, the energy moves to the heart, the fourth chakra. The fourth chakra is another gate that connects us to a larger field of energy—the field of "us and ours." At the level of the fourth chakra, we are not separate as individuals. The heart field is a collective field where we connect so that the energy of the event begins to merge with the unified field of energy. The fourth chakra is a collective state of consciousness that begins to transform the vibration from the "me and mine" perspective of the third chakra into "us and ours," the view of the fourth chakra. The heart chakra is also a place of reverence and acceptance. If the energy continues upward, it moves to the high heart, an energy center where we can express the energy back out of ourselves as service. (Chapter 7 will explore the high heart in more detail.) So the event or the emotion returns to the unified field of energy or into the world. We can begin to use the vibration or experience for an action if it moves to the fifth chakra.

The fifth chakra is the seat of the expression of energy from the first four chakras. It is the energy center that governs expression of the first four chakras through voice, creativity, action, or any other form of expression—even a sigh or a laugh. If the vibration is not expressed there, or even if it is, it can then continue to the sixth chakra, which translates this energy into the form of insight and knowing. Even though we think of this knowing as coming from the head, it is a composite of all the energy that has come up from the root chakra, through the body, into the sixth chakra. From here, the energy circulates back into the body or out through the seventh chakra. The crown or seventh chakra is another connection into the collective energy field around us. We can bring energy in through the crown chakra to circulate energy flow in the body and energy body. This path, bringing in energy through the crown chakra, often is part of spiritual traditions and psychic and mystic work, although most of us can connect at the crown as well.

While the energy is flowing through the chakra system, it is also creating the field for all the organs. I am speaking here just about chakras, yet the organs, blood flow, bones, and skin are all involved in the movement and are being fed by this energy as well. The physical body and energy body are not separate. The physical body is housed within the energy body.

THE CHAKRA MEDITATION

This Chakra Meditation is wonderful for learning about each of the chakras and how to clear them, as well as the different qualities of energy in different parts of the body. This meditation also gives you a chance to deepen your ability to discern energy. Once you can discern energy, you can begin to work with the energy in your body. In addition, this exercise moves energy through each chakra to stimulate better flow through the chakras and physical body.

Before You Start

I like the music "The Chakra Journey" by Anugama (on the CD *Shamanic Dream*), and I frequently use it for the Chakra Meditation.[4] It has a natural progression, and the music clearly changes for each chakra. If you do not have this music, you may meditate silently or use another piece of music. If you use a different piece of music or silence, you will need to have a timer with three-, two-, and one-minute intervals.

If you are pregnant, have asthma, or have cardiac problems, you may meditate while using the hand placements in this exercise, but do not use the rapid breath. Just breathe normally for three minutes at each chakra. We will use the breath in this meditation, but not too intensely. If for any reason this breath becomes too intense, stop the meditation and open your eyes.[5]

The Practice

Find a comfortable place to sit. Relax and close your eyes.

Place your hands, one over the other, over your root chakra (the perineal area, between the legs; see figure 26a). Using your awareness and attention, focus on your root chakra. Stay here for at least two minutes. For the third minute, focus on your breath as well as your hands, and breathe in and out with a bellows breath, allowing the inhale and exhale to be forceful and to take equal amounts of time. Focus the breath into the chakra but do not breathe so rapidly that you hyperventilate.

Place your hands at the second chakra (at the lower abdomen; see figure 26b). Connect the root chakra to the second chakra. Use your breath, hands, and any visualization that is helpful. What you're connecting is the energy of the chakras, and you will feel it when it happens. Follow the same sequence as with the first chakra: two minutes of focusing on the chakra and breathing normally, then one minute of bellows breath while focusing on the hands and the second chakra.

Place your hands now at the third chakra (the solar plexus; see figure 26c). Connect the root and the second chakra and bring them up to the third. Again, use your breath, hands, and any visualization that is helpful to bring the energy from the root chakra to the second chakra and then up to the third chakra. You will feel it when the energies connect. Follow the same sequence as with the first and second chakras: two minutes with touch and regular breathing, and one minute with bellows breathing.

Move your hands now to the fourth chakra (the center of the chest; see figure 26d). Connect the energies of the root chakra, second chakra, and third chakra and bring the combined energy all the way up to the fourth chakra. Follow the same sequence you did at the other chakras: two minutes with touch and normal breathing, and one minute with bellows breathing.

Now place your hands on the fifth chakra (at the throat; see figure 26e). Connect the energies of the root chakra, second chakra, third chakra, and fourth chakra and bring them up to the fifth chakra. Follow the same sequence you did at the other chakras: two minutes with touch and regular breathing, and one minute with bellows breathing.

Move your hands now to the sixth chakra (the forehead; see figure 26f). Connect the energies of the first five chakras and bring them up to the sixth chakra. Follow the same sequence you did at the other chakras: two minutes with touch and regular breathing, and one minute with bellows breathing.

Place your hands on the crown chakra (on the top of your head; see figure 26g). Connect the energies of the first six chakras, from the root to the sixth, and bring them up to the crown chakra. Follow the same sequence you did at the other chakras: two minutes with touch and regular breathing, and one minute with bellows breathing.

In your own time, open your eyes and come back to the room.

THE CHAKRA MEDITATION

Figure 26a: Root Chakra
(Between Legs)

Figure 26b: Second Chakra
(Lower Abdomen)

Figure 26c: Third Chakra (Solar
Plexus)

Figure 26d: Fourth Chakra
(Heart)

THE CHAKRA MEDITATION

Figure 26e: Fifth Chakra (Throat)

Figure 26f: Sixth Chakra (Forehead)

Figure 26g: Seventh Chakra (Crown)

When to Use the Chakra Meditation

This exercise can be used weekly or monthly. I used it daily for a period of four months and found it transformative. I also use this meditation for difficult or big decisions. I find that the different chakras house different states of consciousness or are connected to different wisdoms and answers. They provide different information for when I'm making a big decision. When I'm feeling conflict, this meditation also helps me see where the conflict is housed in the energy body and helps bring the conflicting energies into alignment for resolution.

Years ago, on an impulse, my husband and I looked at a new house. Compelled by the vitality I felt enlivening my lower dan tien when we drove by this home, I set up an appointment to see it, even though my head wasn't considering a different house or making a move. My husband loved the land around the new, prospective house, and we explored the idea of moving.

Even though my lower dan tien was on board, the rest of me was not fully aligned with this move. At the time, I was eight months pregnant, which meant moving when the baby was due. I felt sick to my stomach about this decision, torn and wanting to stay in the house we were living in.

Feeling conflicted about moving and the new house, I went into the Chakra Meditation and posed the question of moving and the idea of the new property to each chakra, noting the responses. At my root chakra, the response was dramatic; the new property elicited more movement and vitality, while the current one quelled and quieted the chakra's energy. The second chakra's response was the same. The third chakra was in chaos or distress at the prospect of moving. The fourth was wide open and lovely, the fifth was more vital with the new property, and the sixth chakra saw me having already moved. The seventh chakra was open to both moving and staying.

I came out of the meditation knowing that the move would be a lot of work, yet I was ready to go because both the move and the new property brought much more vitality for the body. My only issue was fear and the burden of the moving process and its timing; the rest of me was totally aligned. We bought the house. I hired help for the difficult details, we moved, and I had the baby ten days later. After the Chakra Meditation, I never questioned the move or doubted myself.

FREE-FORM ENERGY MOVEMENT

The next exercise is potent for self-healing. I have found similar practices in multiple modalities and cultures. I think it's an accelerated trip into finding one's own healing and one's own direct connection into healing. We first discussed this type of free-form movement in chapter 1, with the story of Keith. Here I want to give you an experience of the potency of this technique. It is wonderful for following the flow of your own body. Your body will begin to do its own unwinding or the movements it needs to do to move energy through the blocks.

Before You Start

You will need a large open space where you can move on the floor without worrying about getting injured. I suggest you do this exercise alone at first—or else around people you are very comfortable with, so you're not self-consciously tempted to stop any movement that the body wants to make come through.

Pick music you like, preferably without words. It can be of any genre, or you can do this exercise in silence. If you have a disability, you can modify this exercise by doing the best you can in a chair.

The Practice

Find a comfortable place to sit on the floor and close your eyes. Keep your eyes closed as long as it is safe to do so in the space you are using.

To get started, raise your right hand and arm and see what they want to do. Allow your arm or hand to move and then let your whole body follow. Move spontaneously on the floor, or move up to standing; whatever happens, allow it to continue. Follow the movement and the energy you're experiencing, but I caution you not to fall into dancing. You may notice you're repeating movements or postures or poses, and that's fine.

Watch the body and allow it to move for the duration of the entire piece of music that you've chosen. Try to keep moving for twenty minutes or so. (You may need more than one piece of music.) You can use different types of music and see what happens. The longer you just allow the body to move, the more the movement will open up.

When you finish, stop moving and lie flat on your back. Rest for five minutes to receive the energy shift in the body from all the movement.

When to Use Free-Form Energy Movement

If you enjoyed this exercise, I would encourage you to do it for an even longer period of time with any sort of music that you enjoy. If you find meditation difficult, you can substitute Free-Form Energy Movement for meditation in your morning practice.

CHAPTER 7

Specific Energy Centers and Targeted Energy-Movement Techniques

I tried to sell this breathing body
To the world, then I came to know
That the body and soul are one thing

—Lalla, *Naked Song*

We are able to target certain symptoms and energy blocks with more specific practices. In this chapter, we will work with specific points in the energy body that I have found especially important for healing: the feet, the hips, the lower belly, the heart, the high heart, and the throat. Three of the practices in this chapter work with points on the back of the body: the back of the heart, the sacrum, and the occiput (the back of the skull).

It is important to work not only on the front of each chakra or dan tien, but also on the back of these energy centers. The energy at the back of a chakra or dan tien can be the most difficult to clear, because the back can hold old patterns, old illness, or unconscious material. In a psychoanalytic paradigm, one would say everything we have not dealt with moves to the back of the energy body, becoming more suppressed and unconscious. From this perspective, the future is manifest from all that we have not been able to handle, so the back energy body can affect how we perceive the future. The back of the energy centers are often neglected or not cleared on a regular basis. We already started working with the back through the Circular Breath and Full-Body Tapping. Now we will tend to the back even more.

BACK-OF-THE-HEART TAPPING

Of all the energy centers, the back of the heart center is my favorite. My interest in this energy center has spurred an exploration of its function in different cultures. I was introduced to this energy center on the back when psychic surgeon Jorge Gomez would operate there for illnesses involved with the blood, like infections or gout, or for serious dilemmas such as life-threatening illnesses, an unconscious death wish, or anyone considering suicide. But I really became aware of the importance of this center when a Mayan shaman slapped me hard on the back of the heart, and I noticed the immediate effect. I went from being spacey or "out there" to being present and clear.

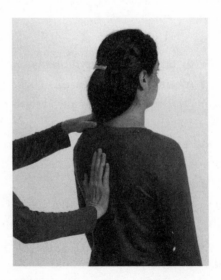

Figure 27: For Back of the Heart Tapping, have your partner use his or her full, open hand to tap between your shoulder blades, the back of the heart center.

The next person I saw work on the back of the heart chakra was a Yaqui medicine man who tapped a client there for fifteen minutes for a soul retrieval. In his tradition, the soul can enter and exit the body through this spot. It is also the site where the assemblage point interacts with the body. As we discussed in chapter 2, the Yaqui tradition of the assemblage point is where all the energy filaments from the energy field come into a person to become sensory data, which is then translated into understanding reality and cognition. In an illness, it is often shifted out of place. Carlos Castaneda wrote, "The assemblage point shifted position under conditions of normal sleep, or extreme fatigue, or disease, or the ingestion of psychotropic plants."[1] Tapping on the back of the heart can affect this assemblage point, clearing it and returning it to its proper place, thus helping with healing.

In the Hindu tradition, the back of the heart center is the back of both the heart chakra and the high heart. Tapping helps chakras empty from the back and is effective for moving out old issues and stagnant energy. At the back of the heart, the body can store energy involved with heart disease, lung issues, and emotional issues.

In TCM, the back of the heart has multiple acupuncture points, including points involved with spirituality (Shendo 10 to 12), the bladder channel (important for energy and chi flow in legs and feet), and the Huanmen points, which are the "gate of suffering."[2] These points address the same energies described by the other traditions.

It's interesting that we use this spot innately in our Western culture. We greet each other with a slap on the back, and we soothe newborns by patting or rubbing here when they are crying. Perhaps we tap here to clear the back of the heart and to bring the infants fully into this incarnation at the assemblage point. I love this energy center, and most everyone I know likes it to be opened. If you've done the Full-Body Tapping practice described in chapter 3, you may have already experienced how it feels to open this center.

Before You Start

This practice requires the help of another person or a handheld vibrating massager.

The Practice

Using your full hand, tap on the back of the heart center, between the shoulder blades (figure 27). It should be firm pressure—as firm as is comfortable for the person you are tapping. If you use a hand-held massager, apply it between the shoulder blades. Tap or massage here for two to five minutes. Then spend a minute tapping all over the rest of the back, starting at the top and tapping all the way to the base of the back. Notice how you feel afterwards, and notice any shift in your breath and chest expansion.

FOOT TAPPING

Working with the feet affects the entire energy body and physical body. This is why reflexology is so effective; foot energy is connected to the entire body. Also, the feet are crucial for connecting to the larger energy field of the earth. Working with them opens the channels that lead into the legs and lower pelvis.

There is data demonstrating that going barefoot decreases inflammation in the body. There is also a movement called Earthing, whose main tenet is that grounding and connecting to the earth increases vitality. While the Earthing proponents use literal energy-grounding technology, they also propose that just going barefoot daily will bring about the healthy effects of connecting with the earth's energy field.[3] I think you can accomplish the same effect by working with the feet.

Some shamanic traditions prescribe Foot Tapping for at least one minute a day on each foot. It is part of shamanic training because the shamanic field uses and responds to the energy of the earth. In addition, it's good for anxiety, previous leg trauma, and knee problems. I think this is a wonderful practice.

Before You Start

In this exercise, we'll tap the entire foot and all its energy points. Don't do this exercise if you've had recent knee or hip surgery and cannot cross your legs or reach your foot. If you have a neuropathy that causes decreased sensation in the foot, you may use a handheld massager on the foot (without heat or infrared) so that you do not injure yourself. Do not do this exercise if you are pregnant.

The Practice

Sit in a comfortable position that enables you to easily reach the top and bottom of each foot. Take your left foot and tap on the bottom and top of the foot using both fists. Tap all over the foot. Focus on the toes, the heels, and the arch. If you notice any tender areas, stay at those points a bit longer. After spending a few minutes on the left foot, switch to the right foot. Tap all over the right foot for a few minutes, as you did the left. Then rest both feet on the floor. Close your eyes and notice any sensation in your feet.

It can take up to a month of practice before you notice a dramatic shift in how grounded you feel immediately after you do the practice. If you add it to Toe Tapping and Full-Body Tapping, you may notice the effect of this exercise sooner.

SACRUM TAPPING

The sacrum, or tailbone, is a gate for the energy flow up and down the back. It is also involved with building and holding energy in the pelvis. Although we discussed the sacrum in the Full-Body Tapping exercise (chapter 3), we will revisit it separately because of its importance.

Sacrum tapping is good for low-back pain and hip and leg problems. It's also important for folks who are very sensitive or for those who frequently feel defensive. The sacrum is a place where we can have an energy block or a leak. We can lose energy from this gate, so tapping to seal it and clear it is a wonderful practice. Tapping the sacrum can also help us stand on our own more effectively. This is also where we're connected into the energy field of a group or a family. If you're having difficulty knowing where you end and where the other person begins, tap on the sacrum.

Before You Start

Anyone can Sacrum Tap. If you have knee problems, you may do this exercise without bouncing up and down.

The Practice

Do this exercise standing. Use your fists to tap right over your sacrum, at the base of your spine (figure 28), while you bounce up and down at the knees. If you have difficulty reaching back to your sacrum, try using a handheld massager. If it's comfortable, you can tap vigorously.

Tap for two minutes, then spend a minute tapping across the whole lower back. Finish by tapping on the sacrum for one more minute. Stop and check in with how you feel.

When to Use Sacrum Tapping

Do this daily if you need sacrum work, or as needed.

Figure 28: For Sacrum Tapping, use your fists to tap right on your sacrum, at the base of your spine.

THE LIVER FLOW

This exercise is named after the liver, yet it moves energy all over the body, making the Liver Flow a good overall tonic. It's also helpful for liver problems, abdominal problems, heart disease, hypertension, anger, and envy.

Before You Start

If you're pregnant, practice Sacred Touch instead of tapping in the lower abdomen. Be sure to look at the figures before you do this practice; understanding it requires both a description and photos.

The Practice

Do this exercise standing. Spend at least a minute on each hand placement.

Place your right hand over the liver area and the left hand on the heart chakra (figure 29a). Using Sacred Touch, feel the connection between the hands and send energy from the hand on your liver to the hand on the heart. Next flood both the liver and the heart area with compassion, gratitude, and reverence.

Move your right hand to your heart and your left hand over your spleen area, on the other side of your solar plexus, directly opposite the liver area (figure 29b). Using Sacred Touch, feel a connection between the hands and send energy from the heart to the spleen. Now flood both areas with compassion, reverence, and gratitude.

Move your right hand back to your liver and keep your left hand on your spleen (figure 29c). Send energy from the liver to the spleen area. Flood both areas beneath the hands with compassion, gratitude, and reverence.

Next, with both hands, tap all around your lung and chest area, including the high heart (see figure 13b on page 56). Moving energy from the spleen to the lungs causes joy to arise, so breathe fully and tap all over your lungs.

Move down to the second chakra area and the area of the lower dan tien (see figure 13a on page 56). Using your fists, tap for another minute. Breathe into the lower abdomen while you tap in this area.

THE LIVER FLOW

Figure 29a: First hand position—right hand over the liver, left hand over the heart.

Figure 29b: Second hand position—right hand over the heart, left hand over the spleen.

Figure 29c: Third hand position—right hand over liver, left hand over spleen

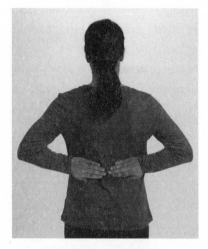

Figure 29d: After tapping on the chest, abdomen, and sacrum, continue the Liver Flow by placing both hands on your back, over the kidney area, and breathing into your hands.

Bring your fists around your back to the sacrum and tap on the sacrum for a minute (see figure 28 on page 134).

Stop tapping and gently place your hands over the kidney area, which is on your back at the base of your ribs (see figure 29d). Breathe into your hands at this area.

Using the fingertips of both hands, tap on the occiput area at the back of the skull (see figure 34 on page 143). Then place your left hand on the occiput area, and place your right hand over your forehead on the third eye. Feel the energy flow between your left and right hands. Now bring both hands to the forehead.

To finish, drop your hands and take a minute to relax.

When to Use the Liver Flow

Use the Liver Flow once a week or as needed.

HIGH-HEART TAPPING

Located in the upper chest area, the high heart is an energy center between the heart chakra and the throat chakra. Tapping on the high heart is a great exercise for asthma, nausea, vomiting, gastro-esophageal reflux, heart disease, hypertension, liver problems, and stomach problems, as each of these may be influenced by an energy block at this location. Tapping on this spot is also an excellent way to move the energies of fear and anxiety, so that instead of staying stuck in the energy body and paralyzing or derailing a person, they can complete their natural flow through the energy body and then flow out of it as action and service.

Before You Start

Anyone can use the High-Heart Tapping exercise.

The Practice

Do this exercise standing. Begin tapping over the high heart (figure 30). You can tap quite vigorously right at the high heart for at least a minute.

Next, using Sacred Touch, place your left hand on your solar plexus and your right hand on your high heart. Send energy from the left hand on your solar plexus to the right hand on your high heart. Then flood both the solar plexus and the chest with compassion, gratitude, and reverence.

Take your hand off your solar plexus and tap on your high heart and your chest with both hands. When the energy begins to move, you may feel a sensation in your throat. If you don't feel an opening in the chest, you can go back and run more energy from the solar plexus up to the high heart. Continue to tap on the high heart until you feel an expansiveness in your upper chest or you until you have tapped for a few more minutes.

When to Use High-Heart Tapping

Use this exercise as needed—or daily—if you have any of the conditions mentioned above.

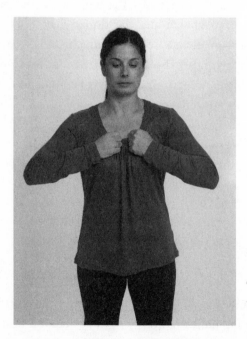

Figure 30: To tap on the high heart, make soft fists and tap on the upper chest, between your throat and heart center.

JAW WORK

The jaw is important for multiple reasons. First, it is energetically related to the hips. We can work with the hips to affect the jaw or with the jaw to affect the hip. I suggest doing both hip and jaw work if you have problems in either area. The jaw is also related to flexibility, not only in the hips, but also in life.

Second, this is a place of receptivity and closing; we actually open and close our mouth in response to stimuli. We can clench our jaw when we feel tense or disapproving. We open the jaw with a smile or a laugh. Picture someone with a clenched jaw, crossed arms, and crossed legs; in this position, the energy body is closed off. When we are interested in and open to someone or something, we lean forward, open our legs and hips, and open our mouths, thereby opening our energy body. The jaw is also where we hold tension and stagnant energy in our face. Keeping the jaw open and loose changes the "face you present to the world."

Third, the jaw is a place of vulnerability, because the inside of the mouth is actually the body's inside. That vulnerability is one of the reasons so many people are anxious when going to the dentist. We close our hips to shut out energies or experiences; we close our jaw for the same reason. For all of these reasons, we need to keep the jaw loose and open.

Before You Start

Anyone can do this activity, although you may notice that it is difficult at first if you have a tight jaw. Keep at it; your jaw will loosen over time. But work only as hard as you feel is needed. If you work the jaw too hard, it will become sore the next day.

The Practice

Let your mouth drop open to a comfortable place. Gently move your lower jaw left and the right in large, side-to-side sweeps (figure 31). Start slowly, then move your jaw from left to right as quickly as you can, continuing for a minute.

Now make your left-to-right movements so small that they are barely perceptible, and continue this small movement for a minute.

Keep making tiny movements with your jaw as you close your eyes. Notice where your primary awareness is in the body right now.

Stop moving your jaw and bring your awareness back to the room.

When to Use Jaw Work

As described above, this exercise takes only a short period of time, but you can you do it for minutes at a time, whenever you feel like it. The reason for small movements is that your jaw will become more sensitive to slight energy shifts. Plus, with small or almost imperceptible movements, you can do this anywhere in public, unnoticed.

This exercise will shift the awareness and energy in your body rather quickly. The more your jaw is open, the more you'll be able to feel the energy flow in the rest of the body, especially in the hips and pelvis.

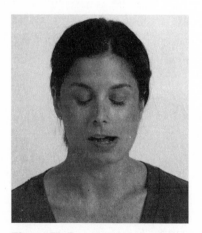 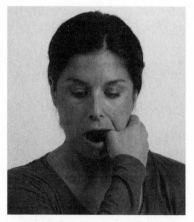

Figure 31: For Jaw Work, gently move your lower jaw left and the right in large, side-to-side sweeps.

Figure 32: To do the additional Jaw Work practice, place your left thumb inside your mouth and your left forefinger on the outside of your jaw. Bring the thumb and finger together to apply pressure on any muscle that is tender or tight.

JAW WORK: ADDITIONAL PRACTICE

This jaw practice has its origins in Rolfing, a form of deep-tissue work. Because we are so vulnerable, at an unconscious level, at the mouth, it is best to do this exercise for yourself rather than receiving it from or doing it to someone else. Be gentle with yourself initially. At most, you may use this every other day. After your jaw is loose, you can practice this exercise once a week.

Before You Start

Wash your hands thoroughly before beginning this exercise.

The Practice

Place your left forefinger on the outside of the right side of your jaw, where the muscles of the upper and lower jaw meet. Take your left thumb and place it inside your mouth to meet your left forefinger (figure 32). Using your forefinger and thumb, apply pressure on any muscle that is tender or tight. Gently press for five seconds on any tender or tense point. Press intermittently, five seconds on and five seconds off, for five or six cycles. Search for all the tender spots on the right half of the jaw, using a fair amount of pressure, and work them with this intermittent pressure. Then switch hands and do the same on the other side of your jaw.

When you are done, take your hand out of your mouth and relax for about a minute. Move your jaw back and forth from right to left a few times, and feel if it is any looser.

EYE WORK

The eyes carry and reflect different energy fields within the body. The right eye reflects the energy of compassion and aggression. The aggression that we put out toward the world and the aggression that we receive from the world affect the right eye and our view of the world. There is less ability to see with compassion when the right eye is wounded by aggression, both our own (what we put out comes right back at us) and that of others. The left eye is the eye of vision and creativity. When we have difficulty with the way the world is coming at us or with the vision we have of ourselves, this difficulty affects the energy of the left eye. When both eyes are clear, we can see with one eye, the Singular Eye—the eye of compassion and vision together.

This eye practice is wonderful for stimulating compassion toward the self. I do this next exercise at the end of a difficult day, on the way to sleep.

Before You Start

Anyone can practice this exercise.

The Practice

Do this exercise lying flat. Close your eyes. Using Sacred Touch, place two fingers from your right hand on your closed right eye and two fingers from your left hand on your left breast, on the nipple area. Feel the connection between the fingers through the body. Send energy back and forth between the right hand on the right eye to the fingers on your left breast. Now flood both areas with compassion, gratitude, and reverence, continuing this flow for at least two minutes. Then allow your hands to drop by your side.

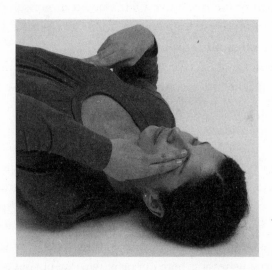

Figure 33: Finger position for the second step of Eye Work: first two fingers of the left hand on the left eye, first two fingers of the right hand on the right nipple. Reverse the position for the first step of the practice.

Move to the left eye, the eye of vision. Using Sacred Touch, place two fingers from your left hand on your left eyelid and two fingers from your right hand on your right breast, on the nipple area (figure 33). Feel the connection between the fingers and send energy back and forth. Flood both areas with compassion, gratitude and reverence for at least two minutes. When you are finished, let your hands drop to your side and come back to the room.

TAPPING ON THE BACK OF THE HEAD

The occiput, the place at the back of the head where the skull meets the neck, is an important center or gate for energy movement. This place is often called the Buddha Smile. It is the point where the energy field connects to the brainstem. You can notice the energetic importance of this spot in meditation if you change your head position from tilted back (closed) to tilted slightly forward (open).

The occipital spot is important for Parkinson's and movement disorders, and for other pituitary and pineal issues because blocks in this area may contribute to these problems. In TCM, the occiput is related to the governing and conception channels in the body, which

Figure 34: For Tapping the Back of the Head, use your fingertips to gently tap on the occiput, the place where the skull meets the neck.

regulate yin-yang balance. It is also an acupuncture point often used when treating depression.[4]

We will tap the back of the head to break up blocks and keep the energy flowing well. Tapping this area also helps disperse stagnation in the head. This is a good spot for moving energy that may be involved in headaches, shoulder pain, and back pain. The back of the head and the third eye (forehead; the sixth chakra) are also important for being able to see what is happening, both intuitively and visually, in the energy field. In shamanic training, this center is opened to help people see the energy field and the energy movement within the body.

Before You Start

Do not do this practice if you have had any recent problems with aneurisms or bleeding in the brain. Be gentle; you do not need firm pressure to tap on this center.

The Practice

Do this exercise standing or sitting. Close your eyes so that you may begin to see what is happening within your inner eye; look into your forehead while your eyes are shut. Also see what you notice throughout the rest of your head while your eyes are closed.

With your fingertips, begin to tap very lightly on the occiput area with both hands (figure 34). Tap gently and see if you can track the energy that is flowing in your head.

Now move down to the top of your shoulders and tap there, right along the spine. Tap back up to the occiput and continue for a minute or so.

Stop tapping and rest your arms. Keep your eyes closed for another minute.

When to Use Tapping on the Back of the Head

Do this practice as needed for headaches, neck pain, shoulder pain, and back pain. You may also use it to increase intuition and to slow down the mind when it is overactive.

THE SACRED GATES FLOW

This practice focuses on three specific gates in the energy body—the sacrum, the occiput, and the crown of the head—as well as the lower dan tien, the body's primary energy center. It is a quick, balancing practice that works on the flow of energy in the back. It brings strength into the back and allows more receptivity in the front of our body.

This practice aligns the body with the mind and third eye; assists the pineal, pituitary, and hypothalamus glands; and is good for many endocrine disorders.

Before You Start

There are no contraindications to this exercise.

The Practice

Practice this exercise standing. Using your fists, tap on your lower abdomen, the area of your lower dan tien, between your pubic bone and your navel (see figure 13a on page 56). Focus your breath into this center as you tap on it.

Figure 35: To finish the Sacred Gates Flow, place your right hand over your forehead and your left on the occiput. Feel the hands connect through the skull. Then tap on your abdomen again to ground the energy movement.

Using your fists, tap on your sacrum, at the base of your spine (see figure 28 on page 134). Focus your breath into this area while you tap.

Next, using your fingertips, tap lightly with both hands on the back of your skull, at the area of the occiput (see figure 34 on page 143).

Place your hands on the top and side of your head, between the ears and crown. Flood the area with Sacred Touch.

Now place your right hand over your forehead, at the third eye, and place your left hand at the base of the skull, at the occiput (figure 35). Feel the hands connect through the skull.

Finish the exercise by tapping on your abdomen, the lower dan tien. This tapping will ground the energy movement that you just did. Then stop tapping and relax.

GIVING BACK

Energy has to be flowing constantly into and out of our energy body. This exercise releases all the energy we've picked up and are storing, giving it back to the unified energy field. This is a powerful exercise for clearing energy when you feel overwhelmed.

In the shamanic trainings, this exercise modulates the unconscious power drive, which is critical if a shaman is to develop beyond using shamanism as a path to gain power. This is also an important exercise for developing a spiritual life.

Before You Start

Although anyone can do this exercise, be sure to adjust the level of strenuousness to suit your physical condition.

The Practice

We'll start this exercise sitting on the floor with our legs crossed. If you can't sit on the floor with crossed legs, sit in a comfortable chair.

Begin by placing your fists into your lower abdomen over your lower dan tien. As you press into your body with your fists, exhale and bend over. Inhale and bring your head all the way up, arch your back, and turn your face up toward the sky. Hold your breath and tap on your lung area (figure 36a). Hold your breath as long as is comfortable and place your tongue on the roof of your mouth.

Next, exhale while you bend over with your hands pressing into your lower abdomen (figure 36b).

Do this cycle again: inhale, body up, face the sky, and tap on the lungs; bend over and exhale. Repeat this cycle two more times for a total of four cycles. On the last cycle, allow yourself to tap on your chest and hold your breath as long as you can. As you bend over at the end of this fourth breath, allow yourself to rest for a moment. With the four breath cycles, you've done one round of the exercise.

Now go back and repeat this cycle of four breaths three more times. You can do one four-breath cycle and then rest, repeat the four-breath cycle and rest, and then do one more four-breath cycle and rest again.

Move into a yoga child's pose to rest for a few minutes: sit on your knees, rest your hips on your heels and your forehead on the floor, and allow your hands to lie palms up next to your hips. When you are ready, come back to the room.

Figure 36a: Giving Back, second movement: Inhale, bring your head up, arch your back, and turn your face upward. Hold your breath and tap on your lung area.

Figure 36b: Giving Back, third movement: Exhale as you bend over with your hands pressing into your lower abdomen.

When to Use Giving Back

I suggest you use this exercise whenever you feel energetically full or overwhelmed or when you sense that your energy is stuck and you can't move it. I use Giving Back whenever I want to express my gratitude for life and for the gift of being alive.

RESTING POSITION BEFORE SLEEP

When the energy in the body is aligned, the body will often heal itself on the way to sleep or during sleep. By "heal itself," I mean that the body will release energy and go back to a natural state of balance. This release and return happens more as your energy channels become clearer and your energy body more aligned.

As I described in chapter 1, one night I had a stiff neck as I crawled into bed. Drifting off to sleep, I noticed my right arm began to shake and move off the bed. I heard a buzzing sound as this was happening, in the ear on the side of the stiff neck. It did this for about ten seconds, then I noticed that a muscle in my neck had released on its own, without my doing any work. That's the ultimate goal of this energy healing work: whenever there is an energy block or an extra stored piece of energy, the body can naturally release it, often on the way to sleep or while we are sleeping. Using this resting position for a few minutes before sleep can encourage energy blocks to release naturally.

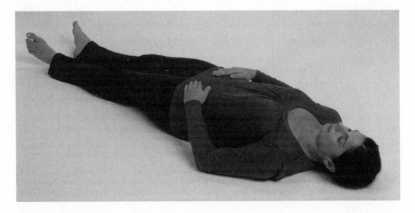

Figure 37: The Resting Position Before Sleep: lying on your back, place your hands on your hip creases, where the thighs meet the body.

Before You Start

Anyone can do this practice as long as you can lie flat on your back. Put a pillow under your knees if having your knees bent is more comfortable for your back.

The Practice

Lie flat on your back in your bed and relax. Place your left hand on the front of your left hip crease, where the thigh meets the body, and place your right hand on your right hip crease (figure 37). Rest here and breathe into your lower abdomen. In this position, the energy flow is in full circulation. I suggest you rest in this position for at least two minutes every night before sleep.

CHAPTER 8

Receptivity

Let your body wear your knowing
Let your heart sing songs . . .

—Lalla, *Naked Song*

Receptivity is what allows us to respond to the energy field within and around us, instead of reacting to it. *Reacting* involves resisting or changing what is happening; in terms of energy, this means we block the flow of an experience through the energy body. *Responding* is very different; when responding, we see or feel what is happening, take a moment to allow it to happen, and then translate or transmute the energy into something else. Responding requires that we be in a receptive state first. *Receptivity* is opening to what is already happening, not only what we want to happen based on personal preference. Brugh Joy used to ask, "What wants to happen?" instead of, "What do you want to happen?" This small shift in focus brings about wonderful results. It softens our edges and facilitates a relationship between our body and the environment. It allows the possibility of new or different experiences to come into our awareness. It acknowledges the naturalness of what is happening to us and around us. It acknowledges that we are part of nature.

Receptivity can happen at the level of the body and at the level of each chakra. When you did the Chakra Meditation (chapter 7), perhaps you were able to feel the difference at each chakra level. Receptivity is a skill, and it takes time to discern different energies. If you had a hard time with the Chakra Meditation, go back and practice it repeatedly until you can notice the subtle difference you experience or receive at each chakra. Receptivity requires that you open to what is informing you at the subtle level of energy. I use the chakras here as an example, yet receptivity is not specific to the chakras alone. Receptivity involves the aura, matrix, dan tiens, and the physical body. Receptivity is the ability to glean as much as possible from the vibrational information presented in the moment, with as little story of what should be or of what happened the last time you experienced it.

Receptivity is the key to nonlocal consciousness and remote healing as well. While remote or distance healing is out of the scope of this book, as you practice receptivity, you may find that your intuition and ability to check in with others from a distance increases.

OUR DYNAMIC, MULTILAYERED ENERGY FIELD

To understand receptivity, you first must get used to the idea that part of your energy field, your aura (or auric field), extends beyond your physical body. Our auric field is constantly in a state of expansion or contraction, according to what is happening and where our awareness is pitched. We can expand our auric field out, in, up, or down, depending on what is happening around us.

When I was a teenager, I read many of the Carlos Castaneda novels about an anthropology student studying with a shaman in Mexico. Stimulated by the stories of the exercises about sensing and receptivity that the shaman gave the student, I would run through the woods at night with my eyes closed for as long as I could stand the fear, and then I would stop. Invariably, when I opened my eyes I would be right in front of a tree I was about to run into. These weren't long runs, perhaps three seconds, yet they were the beginning of my training in receptivity. I knew I could sense those trees. You can try a similar experiment in your home or yard. (If you live in the desert as I do, be careful of cactus—and cliff-side dwellers, please don't try this outside!) Anything alive and animate—plants, animals, and other people, but not chairs, walls, and such—has an energy field and awareness that is communicating with your energy field and your awareness, especially when each of you is within the other's energy field. As Castaneda says, *Inanimate energy* has no awareness. Awareness, for shamans, is a vibratory condition of *animate energy.*"[1]

How we speak, feel, and even desire affects our aura and our relationship with our surroundings. When we are afraid, we often make this part of our energy field smaller and more compact. When we are searching for something outside of us, we can make it larger. In fact, we naturally shift our personal space all the time.

I've experienced firsthand the ability to shift the aura—my personal space, the part of the energy field that senses and communicates with other energy fields—according to where I live or what I need to do in the moment. When my first child was three months old, I went to visit a friend in Los Angeles. She gifted me with a session with a potent energy healer. While I lay on the table for the healing, my friend took my daughter for a walk in the neighborhood. I trusted my friend, yet I was feeling disconcerted about being away from my daughter for the first time. It was overcast in Los Angeles, and I was worried that my baby girl might get cold. While I was on the healer's table, I felt myself energetically searching for my friend and daughter. I could feel my awareness extend out and look around the neighborhood, searching for the baby to make sure she was OK. I imagined where she was, I worried, I tried to send her warmth, and I could feel my energy body extending far beyond the table.

When the healer finished with me, he commented that I had an enormous aura, one of the largest he had worked on. What he was picking up on was an expanded or large aura because of the state I was in, searching for my daughter. I have been on this healer's table since then, and he never again mentioned the size of my aura.

The size of our auric field also depends on who we are and where we are living. Our aura expands and contracts in response to our environment and the space around us. A few years ago, I moved from a house on a large piece of ranch land into a suburban neighborhood, where houses are close together. For the first month or two, I felt the weight of others around me, almost as if I were living with people I did not know. Because I'd lived farther away from people, I think that my energy field was accustomed to being very expanded in an open space; as I adjusted to neighborhood living, I pulled in my awareness to accommodate the smaller lot. While on the ranch, I'd expanded my energy field so that I could feel snakes in areas far from the house; when I moved into a more crowded area, my energy field became smaller, and I sensed the life forms in a smaller radius encompassing the acre and a half I am now living on. While I can still feel snakes at times, it is only within the wall of my new yard.

The same thing happened to my dog, by the way. When we lived on the ranch, she responded to animals that were more than an acre or two away. In the subdivision, she tracks and responds only to whatever is very close to our house. If she were in the same expanded state she was in when on the ranch, she would be responding to the neighbors and their dogs as intruders. She is not even aware of them now, although she is aware of everything on this smaller property and right outside the fence line. I believe she too has shifted her energy field to accommodate the area she now lives in. Doing so may be part of the over-domestication I described in chapter 2, where we lose connection with the naturalness of the larger energy field around us.

Personal energy fields shift and become more and less permeable to accommodate changes in physical space; they also shift with creativity, with ceremony, with techniques and practices designed to pitch one's awareness to a larger field, and even with death. When I was a hospice physician, I was fascinated by the fact that people's energy fields expanded outward as they got closer to death. I would see patients in their homes over time, so I could feel the difference in their fields as they approached death. When I could feel the patient's energy field at the front door or outside it, I knew the time was quite close. I also noticed that the closer to death the patients were, the more they would be disturbed by noises or movements that were farther away because their personal space had expanded out so far. When my father was in the hospital dying, the closer he was to death, the farther down the hall he would notice people. It got to the point that he would flinch and look up as people were coming around the corner at the far end of the hall. An expanded energy field is actually less dense than a pulled-in one, and with practice, we can easily feel the difference in density.

I have noticed that very creative people often have expansive energy fields. I think there is a relationship between the size of their energy field, the density in their energy field, and how much they are in touch with the unified field of energy around them. The less dense the personal energy field, the more the larger energy field around them can penetrate and interact with their fields.

Ceremony stimulates the expansion of our personal energy fields; energy fields of participants are often larger after ceremony and after someone has entered a deep meditative or prayer state. A teacher once told me, "Don't wear your priestess outfit in the airport," meaning, "When you are out in daily life, don't be as open and expanded as you would be during a healing or ceremony."

One thing I have noticed as I've explored receptivity and the aura is that I have become sensitive to being rushed at by someone inside my personal space, which is about three feet from my body. My patients also dislike being rushed at, although how much people are bothered by someone abruptly entering their personal space varies according to their culture. When I worked with First Nations patients in Northern Canada, I learned to walk up slowly and sit near patients for a few minutes before I made verbal or eye contact. Then I could feel my patients open, and I would begin the interview. Contrast this gradual energetic introduction with barging forward with your hand outstretched to greet someone, penetrating their energy field. Your style is your own, yet you may find you can adjust to the person before you with a slow exploration into the space and energy between you.

DIFFERENT LAYERS,
DIFFERENT ENERGETIC INFORMATION

Within the aura there are different layers, and these layers have information stored in them as vibration. These layers have an impact on our relationships, because different information is stored at different distances in our fields. The less conscious we are of something—a thought, feeling, conflict, or belief—the farther out in the energy field its vibration usually is. When I am in conflict with another person, I often move my body to different distances from that person, shifting the personal space between us to shift which parts of our energy fields are interacting. The conflict can be the result of two energies that are in disharmony at one distance and not at another. Begin to notice the amount of physical distance between yourself and another person when you're in conflict versus when you're not. We tend to stay at a specific distance from others when we're in conflict with them, and this distance is related to the layers of our aura. Notice if you are three, five, or even ten feet away from someone when you're in conflict and whether the conflict changes as you move closer to them or farther away. You don't have to tell the other person you're doing this experiment, yet you may glean information about yourself by checking into this.

I introduce the concept of sensing layers of the aura to medical students and residents in an effort to expand their ability to read patients' energy fields and become more open to intuition. In one group, there were two newly married students who were exquisitely sensitive and were crazy about each other. As they did the Full-Body Sensing exercise—which I'll share later in this chapter—they found a place about eight feet apart where they did not get along well or feel good about each other. They were surprised. I moved them closer to each other, and they were again delighted with each other. It was stunning to see their willingness to explore a new love relationship with such openness and energy sensitivity.

At one stage in my exploration of "the space between," I purposely began to sit at different distances from teachers. At one conference I would sit close to a teacher, and at another I would stay as far away as possible from the same person. I realized they have different teachings at different distances in their energy fields. Most of what you learn from a teacher is from the interaction of energy between your field and his or hers.

When I am teaching, I can watch this energy dynamic. One beginner-level student will energetically receive one set of teachings, while a more advanced student will receive something else altogether. I am not actually doing very much *doing;* as long as I am present to the energy field of the participants, the energy teaching happens, and I catch a glimpse of how the awareness is working between us.

LEARNING TO READ THE ENERGY FIELD

Reading the aura or energy field of the body is a skill we can hone with time and practice. Actually, it's an ability we can recover. As I mentioned in chapter 2, we all have the inherent ability to sense and interpret energy fields; we've just been trained not to.

Most animals—in fact, most living things in nature—demonstrate this ability to scan energy fields and harmonize with them. Equine Assisted Therapy with horses is a developing field specifically for training this type of sensitivity. Horses are wonderful at reading energy (as is most of nature), and they respond to it impeccably. The therapy uses the horses' response to help clients and inform the clients of what is happening with them. I have had a horse scan me, and I felt a buzzing sensation as the horse began to read and harmonize with my energy field. Owls also have an exquisite ability to scan energy fields. It is possible to feel their eyes sweep over you as they are using their night vision. I am sure that many of you have had experiences like these with animals as well.

I once had a male client approach me at a workshop, disconcerted because he could not feel energy with his hands. We worked together, and he sensed and felt nothing. I asked him what his hobbies were.

"Hunting," he replied.

"How do you sense a bear in the woods?" I asked.

He shifted, looked me straight in the eye, and said, "I feel the bear with my whole body!"

"Yes," I replied. "You feel energy with your whole body, so why worry about your hands? When your hands catch up to what you are already doing, then you'll sense it in your hands—maybe or maybe not. Follow what you do sense already."

Much of learning to read energy fields consists of widening the aperture of skills you already have, becoming more aware of how you sense and move energy, and then improving how you do it. The following exercises are designed to help you begin sensing information in your own energy field and the fields of others.

YES, NO, AND WOW

We will start with noticing a small expansion or contraction of our own field. This next exercise I call "Yes, No, and Wow." This name was coined by Rita Luque, a daughter of Maria Elena Cairo. Rita once said, "There are only three important words: yes, no, and wow." Words have energy patterns themselves—patterns that are not separate from the body, tone, meaning, culture, or other energy. Thus, words have a powerful impact on our body and energy field.

The Practice

Sit comfortably and close your eyes. Using a loud voice, say the word *yes* a few times. Pay close attention to how your whole body feels. Does your body feel the word? Are you more open or closed? What is happening to your energy body?

Next say the word *no* in a loud voice multiple times. Notice how your body feels. Open? Closed?

Now work with the word *wow*. Say this word out loud multiple times. Notice any sensation in your body.

Keep your eyes closed and your focus inward. Take a breath, relax, and then try all three in a row, "Yes! No! Wow!" After you repeat this trio of words a few times, you will be able to feel a difference with the words.

Come back to the room and open your eyes.

When to Use Yes, No, and Wow

You can try this exercise in any language and see that, no matter what the language, the words *yes, no,* and *wow* carry the imprint of their meanings and have the same vibration in the body. The words are not separate from their energy, and the tone is not separate from the body. So these words have the same effect on your energy field regardless of whether or not you know the language.

The reason I work with *yes, no,* and *wow* is that saying *yes* usually provides an opening and more energy. *Yes* opens us to anything that's coming, whether it's difficult or pleasurable. Opening to something takes less energy than closing to it. While saying *no* is important, often we say *no* to what's happening around us in many unnecessary, small ways. *Wow,* or reverence, opens the energy field and brings in more energy.

Normally when I use this exercise, I'll try it for at least fifteen minutes. I suggest you spend a lot of time with each of these words. It is important to notice the difference between *yes, no,* and *wow.* While *no* is important at the right times, receptivity is a state of *yes* and *wow* more than *no.* After you practice this exercise for a while, you may even notice that you can sense how each word you speak can be an opener or closer—that in some way, each word is a *yes, no,* or *wow.*

FULL-BODY SENSING

This next practice, Full-Body Sensing, explores the art of receptivity. In this exercise, we'll use our whole body to sense the multiple layers in our own and someone else's aura.

Before You Start

This exercise requires a partner. When you first do the exercise, don't spend time translating or deciding what the information or the vibrations you feel mean. Just explore what you are noticing from the level of the body. With experience, you can begin to interpret more accurately what a vibration is, what it means, or what the information behind it might be.

I trust image and feeling more than explanations because each time we move further away from the initial energy, the more our own filters, worries, and fears will distort the information. Maria Elena Cairo used to say, "Even the best is only 80 percent accurate," meaning that even the best reader, psychic, or shaman accurately interprets the meaning of a vibration only 80 percent of the time. The images, vibrations, and feelings are always correct, yet we get caught in our own material when trying to discern their meanings.

The Practice

Stand far away from your partner—about thirty feet apart or as far as the space allows (figure 38). Choose which of you is Partner 1 and which of you is Partner 2.

Both partners soften their awareness: feel yourself open your body, almost as if you are dropping a layer of skin so that you can become more sensitive.

Figure 38: To practice Full-Body Sensing, begin by standing thirty or more feet away from your partner. As one partner moves toward the other, both partners soften their awareness, using their energy bodies to take note of changes in the greater energy field around them.

Have Partner 2 stand still, open to being seen and read by another person. Partner 1 begins to walk toward Partner 2 very slowly. If Partner 2 has difficulty with the vulnerability of being read when Partner 1 is walking up, it's okay for Partner 2 to close his or her eyes.

Partner 1: Notice the sensations in your body and any feelings or images that come into your awareness. When you notice something, stop and feel it a bit longer, then continue to move in slowly. Continue to pay attention to the different sensations in your body and the different awareness at each distance. How do you feel at a given distance? What is the relationship between you and your partner at this distance? Notice how the relationship, feelings, and awarenesses change as you move in closer. Are you welcome at this distance?

See if you can find a layer of protection and defense as you move forward. If you notice one, gently move past this layer and internally ask for permission to move into your partner's personal space. Very slowly, continue to move closer.

When you have come all the way in, make contact with your partner and express your thanks. Spend a moment sharing what each of you experienced.

Next, switch roles so that Partner 2 is sensing while moving in slowly, and Partner 1 is standing still, open to being read.

When to Use Full-Body Sensing

Practice this exercise as often as you can because the goal is do Full-Body Sensing automatically, all the time. I use Full-Body Sensing to connect more deeply with people and to catch some of the unconscious dynamics that are happening between us. You can also practice this with animals and plants. Try it with a tree. I suggest you practice this exercise with a group of friends, taking turns. Another good time to try it is while walking around a supermarket. Open your body and awareness, and see what you notice.

I can connect to people with this exercise as I walk up to them or even when I am approaching from a long distance away. One time, as I was driving to a conference, I opened to and scanned a teacher from 120 miles away, and I continued scanning until I reached the conference. I learned an extraordinary amount in that two-hour drive.

CONNECTING TO THE EARTH

Connecting to the Earth is a potent exercise to allow you to feel the energy field of the earth and merge with it for healing. We're not actually separate from the earth, and this wonderful exercise will help you realize this truth and become more receptive. Because the earth's energy field is quite healing, if you're not feeling well, you can go outside and lie on the ground and see what happens. I do this exercise for at least ten or fifteen minutes.

Before You Start

This exercise is best done outside, lying on a blanket on the earth. If going outdoors is not possible, you may lie on the floor anywhere, even if it's not the ground floor. If you are unable to lie down, you may sit in a chair.

The Practice

Find a comfortable position face down. With your belly on the ground, rest your arms by your side, palms down, or in any position

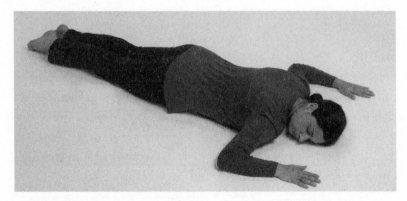

Figure 39: An example position for Connecting to the Earth. While in this position, see if you can extend your energy field about a foot into the energy field of the earth.

that is comfortable (figure 39 shows one position, as an example). Begin to soften and open up your body.

With your breath, see if you can extend your energy field about a foot into the energy field of the earth. If you're in a chair, soften your body and allow the energy field at your feet to merge into the earth. See if you can sense the energy that is radiating out of the earth into your body. Notice the interface between these two energy fields, yours and the earth's. Rest in this position for a few minutes while to you continue to open.

If your head isn't already turned to one side, do so and rest your ear on the ground. If you're sitting in a chair, just pitch your awareness to your ear. Check whether you can hear anything coming from the earth. Now turn your head so that the other ear is on the ground, or pitch your awareness to your other ear, and listen again.

With each breath, see if you can bring the earth's energy field from beneath you into your body on the inhale. On the exhale, see if you can give part of your energy field to the earth. You are softening the edges of your aura and merging it with the field of the earth. Allow your connection with what is underneath you to deepen. If there's anything you're carrying that you no longer want—a heavy worry or pain or difficulty, perhaps—give it to the earth.

When you're ready, roll onto your back. Close your eyes and open your body and the energy field of your back. Again notice the earth's energy field beneath you and sense where your energy field meets it. Bring the earth's energy field beneath you into your body as you inhale, and with each exhalation send your energy into the earth. Take a few more breaths, shedding into the earth anything that you no longer want to carry. When you're ready, open your eyes and end the exercise.

FORGIVENESS

We cannot explore receptivity and energy healing without talking about anger and forgiveness. Anger, the largest drain on the energy body that I know, is often stored very deep in the tissues and energy body. In their tradition of Ho'oponopono, Hawaiians believe that the entire family is involved in an illness and that forgiveness within the family may restore health to the sick person. The illness is understood as an expression of conflict within the family.

When I began to explore forgiveness many years back, I went into a meditation and realized that the answer and formula for forgiveness is in the word. It's a time *for giving*. It's usually a part of your heart or love that you've been holding back because of a painful circumstance. Underneath anger is usually grief. Forgiveness is how we reclaim our humanity, and it provides instant balance to certain aspects of the energy body. It allows the energy body to become more expansive. It's simple to forgive, although it's not easy. All you have to do is let go of the right/wrong stance. Feel the grief, and then let it move through. This is an art that takes a lifetime of practice.

THE METTA MEDITATION

We are going to use the Metta Meditation, one form of a Buddhist-based loving-kindness meditation, to begin to practice how forgiveness feels in the body. Keep the words next to you while we do the meditation.

Before You Start

Choose someone with whom you are having a small degree of difficulty. The first time you do this meditation, you want to make it easy, so you learn the map. After you know the meditation well, you can practice with people and situations when forgiveness is more difficult.

The Practice

Sit comfortably in a chair with the four-stanza meditation text next to you. Once you learn it, you can repeat it with your eyes closed. You may speak the words aloud or silently, repeating the words internally. In the first stanza, we will speak of ourselves, so recite the words for yourself. In the second stanza, bring up a feeling and image of someone you love. Speak the stanza to that person. In the third stanza, invoke a feeling and image of someone with whom you are having difficulty. In the fourth stanza, bring up a communal group that is involved in the difficulty, like a family, a workplace, or all living things.

Repeat the four stanzas below four times each.
May I be at peace.
May my heart remain open.
May I awaken to the light of my own true nature.
May I be healed.
May I be a source of healing for all beings.

Bring into your awareness someone you love.
May you be at peace.
May your heart remain open.
May you awaken to the light of your own true nature.
May you be healed.
May you be a source of healing for all beings.

Bring into your awareness someone you're having difficulty with.
May you be at peace.
May your heart remain open.
May you awaken to the light of your own true nature.
May you be healed.
May you be a source of healing for all beings.

Now bring into your awareness a group, a system, or all living things
May we be at peace.
May our hearts remain open.
May we awaken to the light of our own true nature.
May we be healed.
May we be a source of healing for all beings.

Before you open your eyes, notice any sensation that you feel in your body from this meditation Once you've checked in, open your eyes and come back to the room. Notice if you feel more expanded or more contracted after this practice.

After you have practiced all four stanzas four times, you can put the meditation away until the next day.

When to Use the Metta Meditation

I suggest you use this practice daily for nine days when you are having difficulty with somebody. You will notice a shift in yourself after nine days, and often much earlier. When I first started with this meditation, I didn't agree with the words, but I did the meditation anyway. I found that even though I did not align exactly with these words, the meditation worked beautifully. I thought the other person had changed. Then I realized that something in me had changed to make the other person seem different. That's why I love this practice so much.

CHAPTER 9

Presence and Awakening

There is no Shiva and no Shakti
In enlightenment, and if there is something
That remains, that whatever it is
Is the only teaching

—Lalla, *Naked Song*

Presence is being aware of and responding to the energy field—witnessing, observing, and serving it. I believe that presence is simple: it is being connected in the moment to the unified or shamanic field of energy on multiple levels. As explained in chapter 2, the energy field itself is aware; it is the field of awareness. When we talk about "our awareness," we are speaking about the field of awareness that we have access to at that moment. The more connected we are to the energy field, the more awareness we have access to.

Presence is the quality of being connected to something larger and being centered in that connection more than in the fields of "me or mine," judgment, or comparison. It is asking, "What wants to happen?" and connecting to what is present in the moment instead of asking, "What do I want to happen?" and being disconnected from the moment. Presence is palpable; we can feel when we are connected to the field of awareness, and we know when someone else is, too. When I am making a presentation or teaching, some people say they feel that I can see right into them, that I know what is happening with them. I think they are speaking of presence. While I can often tell what is happening with someone, I do not enter into their auric or energy field to read them. Instead, I harvest the energy from the room (translated as images, feelings, visions, sensations, or knowing) and address whatever comes into my awareness. My eyes are present; they will gaze at someone while I am addressing the issue that has come into my awareness, and often the person is the one from whom the vibrational information is coming. Yet I, Ann Marie, do not connect the image I am using or story I am telling to a specific person in the room because I do not focus my attention on the specifics of each individual. Instead, I allow myself to open to the awareness in the room and go to work with the field of awareness. I allow the presence to work, and I go along for the journey.

When I teach, I keep a notebook with me, because it is often through the teaching that I learn new material. There are connections I make and translations of truths I know that come out only in response to students' questions or the larger energy field's stimulation of an energy that needs to be delivered.

PRESENCE: BEING CONNECTED TO THE ENERGY FIELD OF AWARENESS

As a student, for years I tested how good teachers, in all professions, work with presence. I would sit in the audience of a good teacher, one who was present and connected, and I would internally ask my question. More often than not, he or she would address the question deliberately and specifically.

Once, for example, I had been tracking the word *avatar* (years before the movie *Avatar* came out). By "tracking," I mean that I was paying attention to how the word kept popping up in my life. The first time, I had been driving down the road with some friends and desperately wanted to stop and look at a dress I had seen in a storefront. We turned the car around and went in. I looked at the dress, which turned out to be a size zero—too small for me. Then I looked at the tag—Avatar was the label name. I wondered what the word meant in a spiritual sense and why I was struck by it. A week later, a journal was delivered by mail to my home—a journal titled *Avatar*. Perhaps I had appeared on a mailing list and been sent a free copy. Soon thereafter, the word showed up a third time, so I began to research *avatar* and what it meant.

A little while later, when I was with a Hindu teacher, I sent her my silent question, "What is the avatar stage in spiritual development, and how does one get to it?" I sent this to her as an energy thought instead of asking the question verbally in the group, partly because I was shy and partly because I was testing whether I could send this question and whether she would read and answer it. She looked right at me at a midpoint during the evening and said, "You reach avatar stage when your personal life is the same as your spiritual life, when your personal relationships are aligned with these principles, too." "The principles," to me, are those of energy and awareness, not a typical spiritual sense of the word *principles*.

A dramatic example of presence happened to me with a healer from West Africa. I had offered the use of my house and pool to a friend who was hosting this healer. He was to do an African water healing, so they were going to use my property while my family and I were away on summer vacation. I was sad I was not going to meet the healer, yet I knew I was not supposed to, because the timing was amiss. As I was packing to leave, I felt a tug from my healing room. I went in and did a ceremony to welcome him and offer him all the resources of the land and space for his work. As I was walking out of the healing space, I wondered what he looked like. I also wondered whether he would receive my welcoming ceremony when he entered the room.

Early the next morning, I left for two weeks. When I returned and went into the healing room, there was a card waiting for me, a note from the healer. It told me how he could feel the welcoming and the offering of all the resources of the land and space the moment he entered the room. He thanked me and left a photo of himself. I was thrilled that he had answered both questions. I love interacting with shamans, people with this level of skill, like this: through the field of awareness.

The reason this West African healer and I were able to connect is that consciousness and energy are nonlocal, meaning they are not housed within the body, and thoughts travel out into the field of awareness as vibration. This is why we can often feel or know what is going on with someone at a distance.

I learned from one of my teachers, Dr. Brugh Joy, that I could send him questions from a distance. The first time I did this was remarkable. I sent the questions to him the night before a weekend workshop I was to attend. I went outside, became quiet, pulled the energy up through the root and second chakra to the heart, became as vulnerable as if I were actually sitting before him, and asked him three questions.

The next night, as we all were seated at the beginning of the conference, the room became quiet. Being the extraordinary teacher that he was, Brugh not only answered my questions, he taught me even more through his response. He began to speak to the group, *"Before we begin, I want to address . . ."* and he answered the three questions I had asked. My jaw dropped. Not only had he answered the questions, but he'd also shown me that this practice of asking distance questions works. This became my normal practice with Brugh; I would send my next questions before a conference, and he would answer them during the first night of our gatherings. It was wonderful.

Projecting questions to a teacher is helpful, yet it is really the energy field answering the questions. The student is asking the field of awareness, and the good teacher is responding to the field. Because thoughts are vibration, *anyone* can answer a question we send out; even if we send the question to a specific person, do not be surprised if someone else, out of the blue, answers it for you. Nowadays I send my questions to the field of awareness, and someone or something always steps in to answer, either in the moment or months later. It is the field of awareness we are asking, whether we ask through a teacher's awareness or our own. The field is awake, and tapping into it is how we awaken.

When we track the field of awareness, we are tracking not only it but also our own development and what the field is presenting to us for our next step of learning or awakening. Things become noticeable to us when our psyche is ready for the next level of awareness, and we notice or see something, as I did when the word *avatar* came into my life.

In a conference that Dr. Lewis Mehl-Madrona and I led in Mexico, the concept that the field will answer the questions came up for exploration. How one tracks the invisible field of energy and healing, and how one responds to and interacts with it, was presented for discussion. We were exploring the concept that it is the field of awareness, in conjunction with our own psyches, that is doing the work, not the teacher and the student. The teacher holds the awareness of what the energy field is pointing to for the student, until the student can do it for him or herself. Some of the conference participants began working with these concepts.

One day we were on an outing in the local fishing village, and a Mexican biker gang came by on motorcycles, dressed in leather. One of the bikers had a quote from the Bible on his bike. I quickly copied it, and we looked it up as a group. The quote was from Romans 1:20 and is basically about how most of creation is invisible. Two days later, the group went out for breakfast without Lewis or me. When they returned, they burst through the door. "You are not going to believe what just happened! While we were at breakfast, a man walked up to our table and said, 'Everything that is important is invisible,' and then walked away!" This man was not the biker—he was an English-speaking person who was walking by the restaurant.

Developing a relationship with the energy field of awareness begins with the body and the energy in the body. For many, it starts with a set of teachings, yet the teachings alone are not enough. The teachings are a good start, though without experience, we don't get the insight into realization. I think the path to awakening is faster through the body because the energy facts are easier to learn than a lot of spiritual wisdoms. The wisdoms come from the energy, so once the energy is learned, then the wisdoms become natural action. "Be compassionate" is a great teaching, yet being compassionate can be hard. Connecting to the energy of the heart makes it easy. While we cannot live in the heart center all the time, we can visit it over and over throughout the day.

At any one moment, there is more information coming into our energy field than we can handle. For the information to make sense, we have to sort or filter it. Pitching our awareness to our bodies, dan tiens, chakras, and even different sensations is one way we shift our filter to receive more information or different information. *Change your filter, change your world.* Actually, it is not the world that changes, but the appearance of the world. An approach from a different energy center or filter allows different information to be presented and processed.

The rule here is simple: *the face you present is the face you receive.* The face you present to the field of awareness, a teacher, a friend, a lover, a job, a chakra, is the face you receive back. Ask the field of awareness to teach you, and it becomes your teacher; more information will be available to you.

EXPERIENCING PRESENCE

Although some people can spontaneously experience presence, normally presence is fluid and comes in and out moment to moment. We can augment and facilitate the process of holding presence by using practices to become more clear and sensitive to what is happening and what wants to happen. The amount of presence available to us is directly related to how many centers or states of awareness we can hold at once.

In chapter 5, we began the practice of holding two or three states of awareness at once, which allows for a fuller presence than holding only one state of awareness. Brugh Joy called this "holding two or more states of consciousness." It can also be called accessing more than one assemblage point. The assemblage point is the point of perception, where the field of awareness comes into the body and becomes sensory data. (In chapter 4 we discussed that for the Yaqui shamanic tradition, the assemblage point is behind the heart.)

Moving energy takes two points of focus, so holding two states of consciousness or using two assemblage points (two points of perception) will allow the energy of your own subtle body to connect with energy of the larger field of awareness, allowing our energy to become alive and moving. Holding more than one point enables the *awareness* or the *presence* of the living, awake unified energy field to develop a relationship with us. "Body-full" presence occurs when I am connected to the unified field in at least two major centers, such as the heart and lower dan tien. If I can hold three centers—the lower dan tien (vitality), the heart chakra or the middle dan tien (the collective field of love and awareness), and the upper dan tien (clear vision)—and all three are in sync and connected, the presence is powerful. That presence is what people often feel is seeing into them.

Much of this work with energy and body awareness is designed to allow the assemblage point, the point of perception, to move around, so you can have different experiences of life as you are living it. Moving the assemblage point to the lower chakras has allowed me to move more into the natural world. Moving the assemblage point to the heart has allowed me to move into healing in a wonderful way. Moving the assemblage point to the head and upward allows one to receive and see from a spiritual perspective that is aligned with what we call *God* and *the heavens* in our culture.

Even though our culture has overemphasized spirituality in the upper energy centers, all assemblage points are spiritual; they are all connected to the collective field of awareness or spirituality. In the New Age dynamic, we consider people who have "higher vibrations"—meaning those who are connected to the upper chakras or upper dan tien—to be better or more enlightened, yet this is not accurate. It makes sense that we reach for the higher vibration of the upper chakras because the lower chakras are related to survival, vitality, sex, and death—arenas that the spiritual dimensions disavow. However, *higher* vibration does not mean better or more developed. The higher vibrations are sometimes harder to develop, which may be why we "seek" them in spiritual traditions. Think of a symphony: take away the bass notes, and something is lost. Too much bass, and we cannot hear the flute. Take away the bass notes, the lower vibrations, and we end up in over-domestication, disconnected from the information coming in from the natural world through the root chakra. Although I love the higher vibrations of the upper chakras, we need the vibrations of *all* the chakras. How about letting the whole symphony play? For a start, how about holding three notes of vibration at once: lower, heart, and upper?

As I have already said, one reason we move to higher vibrations is that the lower vibrations, like a bass drum, can drown out the upper tones. The lower vibrations—vitality, security, and feeling—are so overwhelming that we must initially block them out to develop our sensitivity to the subtleties of the higher chakras. With practice, we can attend to multiple vibrations. My wish is that you learn the entire scale, lower to upper, and not hold one in higher regard than another. A good musician plays the entire scale. The heart has the strongest field for healing, so if you focus on only one center, let it be the heart. You can expand your range with time.

I believe that when teachers discuss moving to a "higher" vibration, they are referring to a cleaner vibration—one that is clear and free from unconscious tags or blocks in the energy field or aura. Unresolved conflicts and blocks in the energy body dampen the overall amount of vibration and hinder the flow of energy. This impacts the strength of a person's energy field, which results in a vibration that is not as strong. Also, the size of the aura radiating out from the person is not as large or far reaching as it could be. "Higher" vibration really means a cleaner vibration, with less interference from unresolved conflict.

We tumble here into *direct knowing,* which means accessing the wisdom of energy and the field of awareness with or without a religion, teacher, reader, or translator. While learning this skill and developing direct knowing requires a teacher or guide for certain stages, it can begin with the body and the energy body. Once we learn to read reality at the level of energy, the energy can be our key to direct knowing. Reading the field of awareness begins with tracking reality at the level of energy and the trusting that we are on our way with a direct connection to it. The following two practices are tools for expanding your ability to track the unified energy field and for strengthening your trust in your connection with it.

SOFT SIGHT

Our environment can begin to relate to us as much as we relate to it. Brugh Joy taught me Soft Sight, a practice that can allow much more—and different—information to present itself in your awareness. Although Brugh taught me this technique, you can find it in many spiritual traditions.

Soft Sight is the art of viewing what is around you with a slightly unfocused gaze. You can begin to see energy, auras, or just the mystery of what is in front of you. It takes attention not to focus hard but to allow the thing, plant, person, or landscape to begin to activate. We do this by softening our sight to a glow or soft vision instead of the normal, focused vision we employ for understanding. Soft Sight allows the edges of our vision to blur, so that we don't see details but a softened, less delineated view of what we're looking at. I often laugh at how Soft Sight happens naturally. As we age and need reading glasses, we see less detail and more of the overview, more Soft Sight. Soft Sight is a more expansive view, and what we are looking at can begin to shimmer or shift.

The Practice

Sit quietly and practice looking softly, in a way that keeps your eyes slightly out of focus. Soften your mind as well, by not fully forming every thought of what is. This is a more receptive place of awareness—less filtered and therefore more permeable. Receptivity allows more to come to you from your environment and your surroundings. You may even notice that what you are gazing at becomes more active or alive.

Try Soft Sight for thirty minutes to an hour the first time. I like setting a timer so that the mind does not need to watch how much time has gone by. Do Soft Sight until you feel time stand still, until you feel the relationship with what is around you. Try looking at things in nature as you practice Soft Sight. Then try it with your family and friends. You may be surprised by what happens. Soft Sight is the gate into seeing auras and energy. This is an art, so you have to practice it.

You may notice things begin to shift; you may go into a mini-trance or nonordinary awareness. The world around you may begin to communicate in some way. Don't be surprised. Remember that you are translating vibrations into something that makes sense, so it may seem as if a plant is talking to you, or you may see something in a very different way.

Soft Hearing, Soft Mind, Soft Body

Once you have practiced Soft Sight, you may try Soft Hearing, Soft Mind, and Soft Body, which are similar to Soft Sight.

Soft Hearing is the ability to listen to the flow and rhythm of what you're hearing, as if you are listening under the words. Soft Hearing involves less differentiation, less judgment, less discernment of right and wrong. It is a receptive state. A wonderful example of Soft Hearing is the story I told in chapter 6 of my friend who was on a rant—yet he transmitted healing energy. When you soften your hearing, it is as if you were hearing gently, listening for the energy under the specific noises or tones you are listening to. You want to listen with all your available senses that read energy—underneath the sight, underneath the ears, underneath the mind. Soft Hearing is the key to listening to the field of awareness. Try Soft Hearing the next time you are listening to someone say something that you do not like or that you disagree with. See what other information becomes available to you under his or her words. I use Soft Hearing in my garden to find out which plants need extra attention or water that day.

Soft Mind means spending less time discerning or judging whatever we are perceiving so that we can instead receive an overview of what is being delineated and gifted. Soft Mind seeks overriding patterns of awareness instead of decision-making or judgment, and it is the gate to forbidden thoughts—the ones that shift our thinking into larger containers or structures.

Once you get the hang of Soft Sight, Soft Hearing, and Soft Mind, you can try Soft Body. We began using Soft Body with the last chapter's Full-Body Sensing exercise. Soft Body is the practice of softening the edges of sensation at the level of the body, just as we did in Full-Body Sensing. As you become more comfortable with these practices, you may even find other aspects of your awareness softening.

Learning soft awareness is part of many mystery traditions. In fact, the reason some traditions use certain consciousness-altering plant substances is that they provide such good access to the unified energy field. However, with plant substances, you cannot stop the process at will. Using Soft Sight, Soft Hearing, and Soft Mind, you are able to pull out of nonordinary awareness and return to your daily life when you need to. Again, don't be surprised if the world around you begins to communicate in some way.

FOCUS, OPEN, AND ALLOW

Focus, Open, and Allow is a practice from the four-year training program I took with Brugh Joy. Each of us uses focused attention in our own way; having the structure of a practice is helpful. Once you are able to feel and move energy in the body, you can begin a practice of focused awareness. Energy is conscious; energy is awareness and presence. This practice of Focus, Open, and Allow will allow you to access the direct teachings the field of awareness has to offer. It is done with gratitude and curiosity, with no goal or ultimate outcome desired. This is important. Do not try to *do* something with this practice; instead, use it to learn about things. You may practice Focus, Open, and Allow with things in nature, animals, and even people, yet you will learn only that which you are ready to see. As everything is made up of energy, you can use this practice with inanimate objects, although I suggest you start with living, animate things first.

The Practice

With your eyes, focus your attention on something. It is easiest to start with something in nature, like a tree or plant. Align with your lower dan tien, your vitality center. From this dan tien or from your second chakra, bring up the desire to connect with and learn from your object of focus. Feel your desire or longing to deepen into what you are focused on. This desire is not "I want"; it is literally a desire and longing to learn from or connect with something else. "I want" comes from the third chakra; desire and longing are more primary, coming from the lower dan tien or second chakra.

Notice the energy from your root and second chakra area. Bring it to the heart and let it expand a bit. Then bring it to your head with a focus. You will feel the focus in your eye area and use your eyes to express this energy out of your body. Set it to what you want to focus on in your environment. No attachment here.

Then open your energy field and your body, and *allow*. Open your whole field; experience your body and energy opening like a book or becoming more permeable. Really let go and open up to stillness and listening. Use Soft Mind, Soft Hearing, and Soft Sight in the *allow* portion of this exercise. Quiet the mind and see what comes in. Allow whatever is being offered to enter and present itself. Wait in stillness for five minutes—or much longer if necessary. If nothing comes in, wait longer or do something else. A realization or awareness about whatever you focused on will pop in at some point, often by surprise.

AWAKENING

We hear a lot about awakening in literature and from the New Age movement. The words *awakening* and *enlightened* are used as if we have a collective understanding of them: "He is seeking enlightenment," "She was an enlightened being," "I experienced an awakening," "You feel fully awake." What *is* awakening or being awake?

To an outside observer, being awake does not look very different from not being awake. Being awake is an acceptance of the way the world flows, allowing it to be *as it is* instead of trying to change it. It recognizes that we can change only ourselves and our response to what is happening. We learn who and what we are and serve that process.

Awakening does not always look like what people think it should look like. When you are awakened, you may appear the same as before, yet you've become present to the moment and to who and what you are. It is less about changing behaviors—although change can be involved—and more about being connected to the field of awareness in an ongoing way. Life becomes more about our *response* to what is happening than our *reaction* or desire to control what is happening, because we are part of the entire dance of energy coming through us and around us.

I believe awakening is not a static, on-or-off state. It is not a coin with two sides: awakened and unawakened. Awakening is a continuum that you can spend your whole life diving into. You can become more and more connected to the field of awareness. That connection is not all day or never; it is often a few hours on, then maybe one hour off. It is being connected in two states, then three, then maybe even four, until most of the time you are awake to or connected in at least two centers. Masters stay in the awake state as fully as they can all the time.

As you can keep adding connection points, our position on the awakening continuum shifts over time. What we are ultimately seeking is to be more fully human, from root to crown. There are seven (or more) layers of awareness. Living, truly living, one's life means being awake, as a student, to each layer of awareness and responding to life from each of these layers. When there is conflict, find all the awarenesses possible or present and choose how to live from the larger perspective. As I mentioned with the Chakra Meditation, each energy center is one rung on a ladder of awareness, and all the rungs offer us a unique perspective. You might ask yourself, "Am I awake at the root chakra? Am I awake at the second, the third, the fourth, the fifth, the sixth, and the crown chakras?" Which of our energy centers, our connection points, are awake and present in life constantly varies. For me, there are times when the field of awareness is more present and comes in more clearly, and

I can feel greater connection. There are days when I am not in connection, and then I just go about my day or use a practice to become more awake—any practice that opens the energy flow and puts me in touch with two or more states of awareness at once. Most of the practices in this book can guide you into multiple states of awareness.

Awakening, to me, is being aware of the flow of life and understanding that energy is conscious. When we have this under-standing, we realize that each event of our lives comes in to heal or bring something back to its original wholeness. Wholeness is key. When you are in the flow of energy and connected to the field of awareness and the unified energy field—when you are in presence—awakening occurs, and you will notice that things begin to happen around you. Learn from your experiences. Watch the consequences of your thoughts, not just your actions, as thoughts send out energy too. Stay connected to as many centers or points of perception as possible. Stay open and present, and continue to be a student. The rest will unfold.

CHAPTER 10

Energy Techniques
for Specific Symptoms and
Conventional Medical Diagnoses

Where did I come from, and how?
Where am I going?
Will I know the road?

—Lalla, *Naked Song*

I am frequently asked to make energy diagnoses and prescribe specific energy healing practices based on conventional medical diagnoses. However, conventional medical diagnoses cannot be automatically translated into energy healing diagnoses because the models do not correlate one to one. Even though many energy healers want to say that "this" conventional diagnosis needs "this" energy healing technique, the differences between the paradigms means assigning an energy healing "prescription" is not that simple. One of the biggest misunderstandings or mistranslations I see between energy healing and conventional Western medicine is in the literal transfer of diagnoses.

Western medicine's diagnoses do not correlate with those of energy medicine because these are two different paradigms of health and healing. Each physical body has a different *energy constitution,* which influences how blocks manifest in the energy body and lead to illness. Let me explain each of these concepts in more detail.

If I cannot sit with people and feel the energy in their bodies, giving them an accurate energy healing diagnosis isn't possible, even if they already have a conventional medical diagnosis. This is also true for conventional medicine—a conventional diagnosis cannot be given based on one symptom alone. A symptom or set of symptoms is associated with a list of differential (possible) diagnoses until more information is gleaned through a thorough history, physical exam, and often various types of tests. A heart attack is a great example; people experience the symptoms of heart attacks differently, which is why heart attacks are difficult to diagnose by symptoms alone. In fact, heart attacks are often confused with heartburn, a different disease process with very similar symptoms. We use lab tests to differentiate the two diagnoses and medical imaging to find out the severity.

We all understand the ambiguity about the cause of symptoms in conventional medicine. However, I find that many people, especially those in the early stages of understanding the energy healing paradigm, want a specific energy diagnosis to correlate with a specific symptom or conventional diagnosis, even though this one-to-one correlation is not accurate. The same art of diagnosis applies with energy healing as with conventional medicine: it requires a history and an energy exam or assessment. All the subtleties of the energy body and the symptoms should be taken into account. Often we need to visit a healer who can feel the block, or we must observe our own energy movement and then use techniques, such as those in this book, to get a sense of where the deepest or underlying energy obstruction is. The same way conventional medicine incorporates multiple factors to make a diagnosis, the energy healing paradigm takes into account many different factors, including some that conventional medicine may not.

Another reason Western medical diagnoses cannot be directly equated with energy healing diagnoses is that many physical illnesses are the result of multiple blocks in the energy body, and these blocks are influenced by our individual energy constitutions. As you'll recall from chapter 1, many diseases begin with a single energy block or obstruction somewhere in the energy or physical body. This obstruction, which is never a complete obstruction but a partial one, causes a sluggish flow of energy or a tangle in the natural, healthy energy flow. The excess energy that cannot flow through the energy channel has to go somewhere, so it creates a new energy channel or a build-up of energy in the area behind the block. Over time, one obstruction may cause other obstructions or overflows of energy in the body. Cancers and other serious illnesses result from at least two blocks in the body persisting over the course of one or two years or even longer.

Our genetic makeup and energy constitution play roles in how and what blocks are formed. Originally, we are born with an energetic map that comes from our genetic map (our DNA). The genetics of the fetus are the map for the growth of both the energy body and the physical organs. Some of the expression of the genetic material is affected by outside energy, medications, toxins, and other input the fetus receives in the womb.

This energy map is part of an individual's constitutional aspect, both physically and energetically. Many individuals have an energy body that shows itself to be out of balance when they are under stress. Some people get stomachaches; others get headaches. Some develop sore throats, bladder infections, or jaw tightness. This constitutional aspect of their energy body may show up repeatedly throughout life. Whether someone is born with a particular constitution or it develops at a young age differs from individual to individual. What we do know is that early energy obstructions can set us up for lifelong patterns the same way our genes and behaviors can set us up for future illness. Such blocks are deep and old, requiring a year or more of energy work to work through them and begin to restore the flow to its natural state of balance. These early blocks also affect how the body handles new energy blocks that develop. In addition to our genetic and energy constitution, our lifestyle (including nutrition) and environment play an enormous role in our health.

Because our individual energy constitution, lifestyle, and environment influence how energy blocks develop as illness, we cannot make the one-to-one correlation between specific illnesses and blocks in specific energy centers. Each body also develops unique energy fixes or compensations to handle obstructions, based on the initial energy map or constitution of the individual.

This next story shows how complex and entangled this interface of diagnosis and treatment between the energy and the conventional paradigm can be. One day at the Arizona Center for Integrative Medicine, we invited energy healers from multiple modalities to demonstrate their art to medical students and residents. I had not introduced myself to the group of healers as an MD and fellow energy healer, due to a small glitch in our initial introductions. I've found that such "glitches" are usually gifts, as there are no real mistakes from the perspective of energy and awareness. Knowing this, I opened to what, if anything, the unified field was going to reveal or teach me.

As I walked around to check in with the different healers, I noticed that one woman, whom I did not know, was free. I hopped on her table for a quick session. She was a fabulous healing-touch practitioner.

As our session started, she began to diagnose me. "Why are you not grounded?" she asked. I thought to myself, "Well, I'm organizing this event and thinking quite a bit," as I relaxed and centered my energy in my root chakra and legs. "That's better," she said, and went to work on my body. In ten minutes, she came up with four conventional medical diagnoses based on what she felt in my energy flow. Each time she made a diagnosis, I assured her I did not have that medical problem, and I commented on how wonderful her hands felt. She repeated her Western diagnoses: TMJ, chronic constipation, and two others. "We'll take care of these problems right now," she suggested to me. I repeated that I did not have these problems and also repeated that her hands felt wonderful, which they did. (In medicine, we call what she was doing "hexing"— suggesting to patients they have a diagnosis when, in fact, all the evidence is not there. Hexing frightens people, and the mind is a potent thing. We do not want to suggest a person might have cancer if we are not sure cancer is there, as you can imagine. Still, hexing happens in conventional medicine and complementary medicine all the time.)

Now I was in a deeply relaxed trance state, and I noted that each time the healing-touch practitioner told me I had a problem, I blocked her energetically. I did not want her thoughts about Western medical diagnoses to come into our healing session. When I walked away from her table twenty minutes later, I pondered what had happened. Why so many diagnoses in her healing? What was happening? I thought of my patients who, without Western medical training, could not tell whether or not they had these illnesses. I thought to myself that if this woman had instead said, "I notice sluggish energy in your jaw," instead of "How long have you had TMJ?" I would have had a different experience, and she might have been more accurate.

Then I realized that three of the four diagnoses she had described for me were similar to those I had seen in patients I had laid my hands on in the past two days. Perhaps the energy of those sessions was still present in me—somehow I had not cleared it well—and that was what she was reading. That is another lesson I took away from this experience—that I was not clearing my energy well enough after seeing patients. Knowing there are no mistakes, I worked on the energy she picked up. Her energy reading was likely right, but her interpretation of the energy as particular conventional medical diagnoses was muddled.

Whatever her story and mine, this experience demonstrates that energy diagnoses do not line up in a perfect one-to-one correlation with conventional medical diagnoses. This healer inaccurately assumed that because she felt an energy imbalance, I had a disease process.

If we jump from an energetic to a conventional diagnosis too quickly, we are trying to align two different paradigms. All healing practitioners—energy healers and conventional medical practitioners alike—face the challenge of seeing how the paradigms complement each other without mixing diagnosis models and assuming one-to-one correlations. Once, in my family-practice oral-exams preparation,

I had an exam question regarding a patient who came into the office requesting extensive lab tests because an energy healer diagnosed renal cancer. My task during the exam was to talk about what I would do for this patient. It's normal, when someone hears the words *renal cancer*, to want lab tests to rule out a cancer diagnosis, even if the indications from conventional medicine are not there (i.e., there are no symptoms such as blood in the urine). Part of the art of medicine is to order tests only when tests have a better chance of detecting disease than picking up a false positive. False-positive tests can lead to more tests, biopsies, and all sorts of interventions that can each have complications. So part of what physicians have to do is sort out how to look at an energy diagnosis (or any alternative medicine diagnosis) from the Western medicine viewpoint and reframe it if labs or tests are not warranted. What I suggested, and suggest to you, is that while the patient who wanted lab tests didn't have renal cancer, there was something going on in the person's energy field.

ENERGY HEALING COMPLEMENTS CONVENTIONAL MEDICINE

We can facilitate healing by working with the energy and physical bodies at the same time. In fact, conventional medicine naturally works with both, as well as with rehabilitation, physical therapy, and mind-body medicine. The physical body and energy body are not separate, so when you work with one aspect, you are working with the other. Once an illness or pathology is set in the body as disease, it is wise and useful to address it with conventional medicine, which has wonderful tools to handle diseased organs and issues. Using energy healing techniques in conjunction with conventional medicine speeds healing and can repair some of the energy constitutional issues. I am an integrative medicine physician, so I use energy healing, botanicals, nutrition, exercise, and mind-body techniques, and I refer my patients to TCM, homeopathy, manual medicine, and ayurvedic practitioners.

Once symptoms or illness are present, there are enough similarities between energy diagnoses and Western diagnoses that we can prescribe specific energy work to address the *probable* energy blockages involved. People often mistakenly equate a Western diagnosis with a particular energy block in the body. While it is true that there are *commonalities*—certain diseases often stem from blocks in particular areas—the energy blocks also may be in several different spots. As an example, foot pain can be the result of a block in the foot, knee, or hip. You must remember to look at and work with the constitution and history of your own body and energy body. Please keep this in mind as you read the rest of this chapter. When I'm speaking of the blocks that underlie a particular illness or condition, I'm speaking only of *probable* blocks, and the suggested practices allow you to work with the *probable* areas affected. You may start using the energy healing practices suggested for a specific symptom, illness, or condition, but then you have to explore your own energy body for yourself. Going to see an experienced energy healer, along with an experienced TCM practitioner, will help in this process; these two healers will look at different layers of the energy body and give you a full perspective.

Conventional medicine and energy medicine are *complementary* modalities and need to be treated as such. Use all the modalities of health and healing at your disposal, and for symptoms that are worrisome, use conventional medicine as an ally and guide. While it is possible to transform disease at the level of energy or consciousness, doing so is very deep and difficult work, and it requires grace as well as skill. The skill of transforming serious physical illness through energy and consciousness alone is not always available to even the most adept master.

I want to tell you one story to show you how challenging it is to become totally adept at healing serious illness with energy and consciousness alone in a reproducible fashion. In one shamanic tradition, the ultimate initiation is to lie in a pit with rattlesnakes. Rattlesnakes respond to fear and aggression, so the initiate must stay heart centered. If the initiate is bitten, he or she must immediately move into the body and follow the venom energetically to accept it and transform it through energy and consciousness. The initiate stays in this pit until the snakes die, the initiate dies, or the snakes stop rattling for days and are quiescent. When students in this shamanic tradition successfully goes through this initiation, they have all the tools necessary to reliably transform disease with energy, and they can call themselves a shaman in the most advanced sense. Can you imagine? This is not easy work.

I have seen people transform *serious disease* through consciousness and energy alone—sometimes spontaneously and sometimes without shamanic training—however, these cases are the exception, not the rule. Do not rely on the fact that complete healing with energy alone is possible. I have had many clients come to me to work with energy only—patients with life-threatening diagnoses who have left conventional medicine—but they lack the skill, grace, and training to actually do the work it would take to transform the disease through energy and consciousness alone. As a practitioner of multiple modalities, it breaks my heart to watch how they have chosen one modality over another when a combination might get them through the disease and keep them alive.

Now that I have laid out the complementary nature of energy and conventional medicine, we can explore some common, general connections between energy blocks and conventional diagnoses and attempt to work with the energy body for specific conventional diagnoses. Fortunately, none of these exercises is harmful, and the serious contraindications are stated, so it's OK to use them even if they don't address the primary block in the body. They may address secondary blocks that have occurred as a result of a primary block.

I have put together energy regimens that you can use to work with specific symptoms, diseases, and conditions. You will want to incorporate these exercises into an integrated healing approach that can also include nutrition and diet, supplements, physical exercise, mind-body medicine, massage, physical and chiropractic therapy, traditional Chinese medicine, manual medicine, and a spiritual practice, as well as conventional medicine.

Try the recommended practices over the course of a month. If you notice pain or problems increasing with the use of these practices, discontinue them for a week or so. Once the pain or difficulty has subsided, you can return to the practice slowly and gently.

Please see a primary-care physician for any medical problems before you decide to work with energy alone. I cannot stress this enough.

In order to recommend specific energy practices without making direct, one-to-one comparisons to conventional diagnoses, we will look at the body through broad disease categories and organ systems. I've suggested a set of practices to work with a particular body area or disease process, as well as with the surrounding areas and important energy flows.

ENERGY PRACTICES FOR PAIN

As we discussed in chapter 1, pain is a result of blocked energy. There is too much energy going through a channel or area that is constricted. This disruption in the energy flow happens in conjunction with other factors in the physical body, such as overuse, trauma, inflammation, infection, and toxins. Again, the conventional diagnosis must be explored first, especially with new-onset pain. For example, shoulder pain can have multiple causes, from a shoulder injury to referred pain from other locations, such as chest pain (angina), gallstones, or even pneumonia.

There is also pain that occurs from dysfunction in the brain; we call this "centrally mediated pain." Dealing with this type of pain is beyond the scope of this introductory book. However, if you have centrally mediated pain, I suggest you use the breath practices, Shaking the Bones, and the meditation practices as often as you can.

We don't want to just add more energy into a painful area because that area may already have too much energy flowing through it, and adding more will increase the pain. Instead, we want to move the energy through the block or away from the site of pain. Let's say someone has an old ankle injury; it's mostly healed, but the pain comes back with exercise or in certain types of weather. Toe Tapping may initially cause a bit of pain in the ankle, because the tapping is adding energy into a system that has partially shut down in order to accommodate an energy obstruction. The body may have turned down the flow in the leg the same way one might turn down the water pressure to accommodate a constricted pipe. However, continuing to use Toe Tapping in a gentle fashion over time will allow the residual block from the old injury to clear. The ankle will no longer have flare-ups or residual pain, and the body will have access to more energy flow overall. You may find this pattern happens in many parts of the body when you use energy healing exercises.

First, we'll talk about acute pain, then we'll address different types of chronic pain that reoccur in specific areas.

Acute Pain

First find out what is physically causing the acute pain and get the appropriate medical care. If you know for sure that the underlying acute issue doesn't require medical care, you may use energy healing practices to open the block in the energy body and move the energy through the area. Because acute, new-onset pain is linked to a corresponding recent block, it is best not to add energy right into the area; instead, work farther up on the body. For example, some foot pain gets better when you work with the hips, which allows more energy to flow from the foot up through the leg, through the hip, and into the body's energy system in the torso. This pattern of energy obstruction holds true for most acute pain.

To try to immediately relieve pain, try using the Pain Drain Technique described below. If you have an acute trauma like a broken foot or knee, then I suggest using both conventional and energy therapy. Get the bones set and then do the practices once you are able to move the limb.

The Pain Drain Technique

This technique can be used for acute pain in one area or joint. Put your left hand over the area of the acute pain. Allow your right hand to rest off your body, toward the floor. Use breath and visualization to help the excess energy drain out of the painful area and into your left hand, then from your left hand through your body into your right hand, and then from your right hand out of the body. On your inhale, breathe the energy from the painful area into your left hand, and on the exhale use your breath to visualize the energy flowing out of your right hand and onto the floor. You're using your hands like a hose or siphon, allowing the excess energy a place to discharge out of the body. Do this until the pain begins to subside.

Next, use the Circular Breath (described on page 94) to move the energy in a flow around the body.

If necessary, you can use the Pain Drain Technique while you're waiting to get medical care for the underlying cause of the pain.

Acute Pain from a Muscle Strain

If you experience an acute muscle strain, it is best to move the energy through the corresponding block quickly. Try the Pain Drain Technique, the Circular Breath, and then Shaking the Bones. If Shaking the Bones causes more pain, stop and reassess. You may need to rest and try it again the next day. Using a handheld vibrating massager can also be useful for moving energy through the area.

Back Pain

Acute back pain can come from many places, including an injury to the muscles, vertebrae, or ribs; disc protrusion or nerve impingent; or problems with the lungs, kidneys, heart, pancreas, or other abdominal organs. If you have acute back pain, follow the suggestions of the previous section on acute pain.

If you have chronic back pain, you may use the techniques described below. If you know your back and are sure you just mildly reinjured it, then the initial energy cause that made the system weak can be addressed. Use these practices in conjunction with the appropriate conventional-medicine techniques for your diagnosis.

For chronic low-back pain, you need to help the flow of energy up the back, and you often need to open the hips and legs, too. Use the exercises listed below during your back-pain episode—as much as you can easily tolerate. Using the exercises when you are pain free is also very important. Opening the channels and energy flows when you are pain free actually can prevent the pain from flaring up by increasing the amount of energy that can flow through your energy channels. Using the exercises when you are pain free increases your ability to hold and move energy in your body.

Use Sacrum Tapping, Shaking the Bones, the Heart Center Meditation, and the Sacred Gates Flow daily. If this is too much to do in one day, do half of the practices on Day One and the other half on Day Two. Use Toe Tapping while lying flat in bed if you can tolerate it. Also begin to do some gentle yoga, and I suggest you receive a series of six to twelve massages.

Hip Pain

Once you have been looked at by a primary-care practitioner and either received conventional-medicine recommendations or been cleared medically, use the exercises below. If you have had a hip replacement, please check with your orthopedic physician before using Toe Tapping.

The hips are crucial for the energy body because the hips house the gate that allows energy to come up the legs into the body. For chronic hip pain, like chronic low-back pain, hip opening is important.

Use Shaking the Bones and Toe Tapping daily; I suggest you do the Toe Tapping in bed. Follow it immediately by the yoga pigeon stretch, if you are able. I would also do Full-Body Tapping, focusing on the hips and sacrum area, at least every other day.

Use the Circular Breath daily or every other day to help the energy flow up the back. Jaw Work is also very important in hip pain. Do the jaw exercises from chapter 7 every two to three days.

Knee Pain

Acute knee pain can be a serious problem, so have it checked with your primary-care practitioner. Once it is clear you do not require an acute medical intervention, then knee pain is similar to hip pain, and you can use the energy techniques recommended above for hip pain to complement your conventional medical care. Skip the pigeon stretch if it causes you more knee discomfort.

Neck Pain

New-onset neck pain must be looked at with a neck exam and imaging, like a neck x-ray. Once you are cleared medically, you may use the practices below.

Use Shaking the Bones daily, to loosen the energy blocks in the neck. Make sure you let the head loosely drop forward, so the weight of the head stretches the neck and the energy can begin to flow. Also use the Circular Breath, the Sacred Gates Flow, and the Heart Center Meditation daily. I also suggest some massage and craniosacral work by a good practitioner.

Headaches

In both the energy paradigm and the conventional-medicine paradigm, headaches occur for a variety of reasons. In addition, there are different types of headaches. So have new-onset headaches and chronic headaches checked out medically.

During a one-sided headache, do Eye Work while you use the Circular Breath. First, place two fingers on your closed eyelid on the painful side of the head and two fingers from the other hand on the opposite breast. (For example, for a left-sided headache, place two fingers on the left eyelid and two fingers on the right breast.) With your breath as one focus point and your hands as another, move energy from the eye to the opposite breast. Visualize the energy flowing from the affected side of the head through the heart chakra to the breast. After about five minutes of this flow, practice Toe Tapping for a few minutes, and then go back to Eye Work while you concurrently practice the Circular Breath.

If you can tolerate Shaking the Bones while you have a headache, give that exercise a try. You may also use Connecting to the Earth.

For headaches that occur on both sides of the head, try to run the energy from the head down into the second chakra and heart chakra. Place your hands on your second chakra and see if you can breathe into the lower abdomen with the Abdominal Breath. Also use Eye Work to run energy from each eye down to the opposite breast and side of the chest. Finally, run the energy from the head to the heart chakra. You may also use Connecting to the Earth.

If you suffer from chronic headaches, be sure to work with the energy body when you do *not* have a headache. You will have better results with the above techniques if you do, and you want to make sure the energy body is grounded. To work with chronic headaches, use Shaking the Bones daily. As time permits, daily or every other day, use Toe Tapping, Sacrum Tapping, Tapping on the Back of the Head, the Sacred Gates Flow, Eye Work, the Liver Flow, and the Heart Center Meditation. Use Jaw Work weekly until your jaw is loose. Practice Soft Sight, Soft Hearing, Soft Mind, and Soft Body as often as you can.

Abdominal Pain

Like other types of pain, abdominal pain can have many causes, some of which require immediate care. For abdominal pain that is mild or is due to irritable bowel syndrome or treated inflammatory bowel disease, you may use the following practices.

Place your hands on your abdomen and use Sacred Touch to run energy into your abdomen. While adding energy this way runs counter to much of the pain advice I have given so far, in the abdomen it can stimulate relaxation. Also use the Abdominal Breath and the Circular Breath during an episode of pain—and daily when you do not have pain. When you are pain free, use the Liver Flow daily, as well as Full-Body Tapping as often as you can. Use the Resting Position Before Sleep every night.

Fibromyalgia Pain

Fibromyalgia is a special case with energy medicine. In fibromyalgia, there is an overwhelming dampening of the body's vital energy, and large influxes of energy can cause a flare-up of symptoms. Many people with fibromyalgia notice that after a healing session or a wonderfully vital day, they experience heightened symptoms for the next day or so. With fibromyalgia and other full-body pain syndromes, it is important to add in and move the energy in the body very slowly. All of the practices should be modified so they're used for only a few minutes a day initially. It is important to do a two- or three-minute session every day and then add one or two minutes to each session per week. Fibromyalgia responds well to energy practices as long as you're consistent with daily practice and bump up the time slowly. Practice energy healing patiently and consistently, and you can expect to see a major shift in your body over six months.

For daily use, begin with a two-minute practice of Toe Tapping, Shaking the Bones, or Full-Body Tapping (tapping on each part of the body for ten seconds or so), alternating between them each day. Then use the Heart Center Meditation for at least five to ten minutes each day. Finally, practice the Circular Breath daily for three to five minutes. Each week continue to alternate the practices and increase the length of your practice by one minute. Continue to practice the Circular Breath daily for three to five minutes per day. Use the Resting Position Before Sleep each night.

In addition, use the Full-Body Energy Connection (the full-length practice is fine) weekly. Giving Back, Jaw Work, Eye Work, and Connecting to the Earth can be done weekly.

SUGGESTED ENERGY PRACTICES FOR SPECIFIC ILLNESSES AND CONDITIONS

This section lists specific medical issues, or categories of issues, that I see most commonly in my integrated healing practice and that respond very well to energy healing in combination with other types of care. If you want to use energy healing for a specific concern not listed here, I recommend you use the practices as I have delineated them in each chapter, and pay attention to what happens to your energy flow and your symptoms. You may want to visit an energy healer in your area for advice concurrent with your conventional medical care.

Anxiety

New-onset anxiety or panic attacks need to be checked by your primary-care practitioner to ensure they are not stemming from a problem in the endocrine system. Once you are sure that you do not have an underlying conventional-medicine issue, anxiety and panic attacks respond well to energy practices. As we discussed earlier, the nervous system can be retrained with energy practices, often treating the root cause of the anxiety. Initially, you need to use the practices when you are not anxious. You may also use the practices when you are experiencing the anxiety, if you can. Over a month or so, you will find that you can use the practices with ease once you notice the anxiety rising.

Use Toe Tapping daily for ten minutes in the morning, followed by the Heart Center Meditation for at least five minutes. Use Toe Tapping again for five minutes in the afternoon. Use the Abdominal Breath as often as you can throughout the day. Use the Circular Breath and Giving Back daily as well. Weekly or more often, use Connecting to the Earth; Full-Body Sensing; Shaking the Bones; Free-Form Energy Movement; and Focus, Open, and Allow.

Autoimmune Disease

This broad category is difficult to address because each autoimmune disease is different. Any autoimmune disease should be managed first by a conventional medical practitioner. You may use the practices below as an addition to your treatment.

Daily, use Toe Tapping, High-Heart Tapping, Back-of-the-Heart Tapping, Eye Work, and the Heart Center Meditation. Practice the Abdominal Breath as much as you can throughout the day. Weekly or more often, use the Chakra Meditation, the Metta Meditation, the Full-Body Energy Connection, Connecting to the Earth, and Free-Form Energy Movement.

Cancer

Energy prescriptions for cancer depend on the type of cancer diagnosed. This is important. Due to the variety of types of cancer, I cannot give a full plan here; however, I will give a few guidelines.

A cancer diagnosis requires a complete opening of each chakra and a complete exploration of the energy body. Healing at a very deep layer is required. This healing naturally happens through the process of conventional medicine treatment, yet will be augmented by adding energy practices. These practices can also help during chemotherapy and radiation therapy, if you are up for doing them. *It is important that you use very light pressure for any of the tapping practices.* We want to move the energy in the body with direct body tapping, but in a gentle way.

Practices to use daily include Full-Body Sensing, Toe Tapping, High-Heart Tapping, and the Heart Center Meditation. In addition, if you are feeling strong enough while you are receiving chemotherapy, use Shaking the Bones, Giving Back, and the Liver Flow daily. Use the Resting Position Before Sleep each night. On alternate days, use Full-Body Tapping with light pressure.

At least weekly, use the Full-Body Energy Connection; the Chakra Meditation; Yes, No, and Wow; Connecting to the Earth; Soft Sight, Soft Hearing, Soft Mind, and Soft Body; Focus, Open, and Allow; and any of the specific practices that are related to the area of the body where the cancer is located. Again, use light pressure for all the tapping exercises.

Chronic Fatigue

Chronic fatigue syndrome is different than fatigue or not having enough energy. Chronic fatigue is a deep conflict housed in the body and requires slow, patient energy work. As with fibromyalgia, a large influx of energy can cause a flare-up of symptoms, so you have to shorten the practices. Use each recommended practice for two to three minutes a day at first and increase the time by one minute a week.

For your daily practice, begin with two to three minutes of Toe Tapping or Shaking the Bones, alternating between the two each day. Use the Heart Center Meditation daily for at least five minutes. Every other day, use a shortened version (five minutes) of Full-Body Tapping. Each week, continue the practices, but increase the length of your practice by one minute. Use Connecting to the Earth daily, even if you experience a flare-up of symptoms. Use the Resting Position Before Sleep every night for two to three minutes.

Practice the Chakra Meditation, in its full length, every week, but without the rapid breathing. After a month, use the Chakra Meditation daily, if possible, but do not add the rapid breath for another month. Then, if you tolerate the breathing, use the Chakra Meditation with the breath daily.

Also use the Full-Body Energy Connection weekly. This practice is gentle enough to use in its full form. Use Full-Body Sensing weekly if you can tolerate it—meaning if it feels as if it is assisting you instead of creating flare-ups.

Depression

New-onset depression needs to be checked out by your primary-care practitioner to see if it is the result of a serious organic medical cause, such as a brain, blood, endocrine-system, or other physical issue. **If you feel suicidal, seek immediate help.** Tell someone if you start having intrusive thoughts about ending your life. Once you are clear that you are experiencing a standard depression, you can use the practices below.

In depression, there is a loss of vital energy. To recover that, you have to reconnect to your vital energy and lower dan tien. This is tough, because depression robs us of the energy and motivation to do practices that will bring in vital energy and pull us out of the depression. The easiest energy-moving practice to do is any form of exercise you love. If you can do only one thing, exercise. In addition, try the practices in the following paragraphs. I urge you to find a way to use them each day. Ask a friend to visit you daily and do the practices with you, if that helps you do them regularly.

Every day, do five minutes of Toe Tapping, five minutes of Shaking the Bones, and at least ten minutes of Full-Body Tapping, spending extra time (at least two minutes) tapping on the back of the heart. Use a handheld massager to reach this spot if you do not have someone to tap it for you. In addition, tap your armpits for two minutes on each side, with your hand literally in your armpit. Practice the Metta Meditation every day, focusing on forgiving yourself and other people in your life, one by one. Start with forgiving yourself.

Use Giving Back, the Liver Flow, and Connecting to the Earth every other day or at least weekly, as time permits. Use the Heart Center Meditation every day, if you have any extra time. Use the Resting Position Before Sleep each night. It is worth putting quite a bit of time into these practices so that you can return to life in a vital way.

Gastro-Esophageal Reflux and Other Stomach Problems

Because the symptoms of reflux can be so similar to angina or cardiac chest pain, have your symptoms checked by a primary-care practitioner to rule out heart problems or any other serious problem in your upper abdomen. Once you are cleared, use the following exercises daily when you are pain free: the Liver Flow, High-Heart Tapping, Back-of-the-Heart Tapping, Giving Back, and the Heart Center Meditation. Weekly, use Full-Body Tapping, Connecting to the Earth, and the Chakra Meditation.

Fatigue

Because fatigue or exhaustion can come from a variety of medical conditions, first see your primary-care practitioner to make sure yours is not caused by anemia, a thyroid problem, or another issue. Once you are clear that your fatigue does not need conventional treatment, use the following practices. You may also use the practices along with conventional treatment.

Fatigue comes from not having enough energy gathered in the lower dan tien or from having too many leaks in the energy system. To deal with fatigue, we need to open the energy flow in the legs and hips, gather energy every day, clear old blocks, and work with any potential leaks in the energy system.

Use Toe Tapping first thing each morning. Then use Full-Body Tapping and spend extra time tapping on the lower dan tien, hips, and sacrum. Next use Shaking the Bones. Then use the Circular Breath for at least three minutes. Finish your morning practice with the Heart Center Meditation. Make this morning practice at least a half hour each day.

When you notice fatigue during the day, use Toe Tapping and Shaking the Bones. You can also tap on the lower dan tien and hips. You can develop a five-minute routine that incorporates all three of these. You may find you need to practice this routine multiple times a day. Also use the Abdominal Breath and the Root Chakra Breath multiple times during the day, enough so that they become second nature.

In addition, weekly use Jaw Work, Eye Work, High-Heart Tapping, Foot Tapping, and Giving Back.

Heart Disease

Heart-disease care must be managed by a conventional-medicine practitioner. Use the following practices in conjunction with your conventional care. Daily, use the Heart Center Meditation, the Liver Flow, Back-of-the-Heart Tapping, High-Heart Tapping, and the Metta Meditation. Alternate Shaking the Bones, Toe Tapping, and Full-Body Tapping, using one for at least five minutes each day. Weekly, use Eye Work, the Full-Body Energy Connection, the Chakra Meditation (without the rapid breath), and Connecting to the Earth. Practice Full-Body Sensing whenever you can.

Hypertension

Hypertension needs to be managed medically. Use the practices below in addition to any conventional medical management you receive. Hypertension, from an energy perspective, is usually caused by too much energy flowing through an energy system that is too constricted. You have to open all the channels in the body.

Daily, use Shaking the Bones for ten minutes and the Heart Center Meditation for ten minutes. Also use Back-of-the-Heart Tapping and Eye Work daily. Practice the Abdominal Breath as often as you can throughout the day, until you find you are using it naturally most of the time. Weekly or more often, practice Yes, No, and Wow; Giving Back; and Connecting to the Earth.

Injuries and Wounds

As explained in chapter 1, when we incur an injury, wound, or other trauma, the physical problem and the energy block occur at the same time, and both need to be addressed. The physical body naturally heals in conjunction with the energy body; however, sometimes the energy flow remains interrupted for years after the physical body has apparently healed. Think of a broken ankle. Once the bones heal, people often find their ankle is weaker than it was and that it begins to hurt when fatigued or even in certain types of weather. In these situations, there is a sluggish energy flow in the ankle, which still needs to be worked with after the bones have healed.

Traumatic injuries and wounds require supportive care and rest initially. If the wound or injury is painful, use the Pain Drain Technique, described earlier in this chapter, to remove energy from the area after you have sought conventional treatment for the wound or injury. Also use the Circular Breath to help decrease the pain.

Once the pain has subsided and the injury has begun healing (days later), use the Full-Body Energy Connection to run energy around and through the wound or area of trauma, focusing on the joints on both sides of the wound. For example, if you break your elbow, run energy from the wrist to the shoulder. If this increases the pain in the injured area, stop and wait a few more days before resuming the energy practice. Be sure not to move the joint or area if it requires immobilization! In addition, try doing Shaking the Bones very gently every day to keep your entire energy system vital and to enhance its energy flow after a few days of rest.

Leg Neuropathy, Restless Leg Syndrome, and Insomnia

I have grouped these three diagnoses together because they respond to the same energy exercise for treatment, albeit for different reasons. Leg neuropathy, restless leg syndrome, and insomnia respond very well to energy exercises. If you have numbness in your feet, do not use Toe Tapping, because you aren't able to regulate how hard you're tapping. Instead, use a handheld massager to stimulate the flow in your toes, legs, and hip, so you can observe what you are doing and avoid injury.

Otherwise, use Toe Tapping for five to ten minutes each morning. Nightly, use Toe Tapping again for at least five minutes in bed and then use the Resting Position Before Sleep as you drift off to sleep. Use Toe Tapping again for a minute or two if you wake during the night from your symptoms.

Liver Problems

In addition to the conventional medical care you are receiving, I suggest you see a TCM practitioner and use these practices: daily, use Toe Tapping, the Liver Flow, Giving Back, the Sacred Gates Flow, and the Heart Center Meditation. Weekly, use the Full-Body Energy Connection and Free-Form Energy Movement. If you have a liver issue that interferes with normal blood clotting, use *very* light tapping when you work with the Liver Flow.

Respiratory Problems

Chronic respiratory problems require conventional medical care. Use these practices along with the medical care you are receiving: daily, use Full-Body Tapping, High-Heart Tapping, Back-of-the-Heart Tapping, the Liver Flow, and Eye Work. Weekly or more often, use Toe Tapping and Giving Back.

Rheumatoid Arthritis and Osteoarthritis

While these forms of arthritis have different causes, you may use these practices to assist with the energy flowing through the joints: daily, use Shaking the Bones and the Heart Center Meditation. Every two or three days use Full-Body Tapping, the Full-Body Energy Connection, and Connecting to the Earth.

Skin Problems

Daily, use Shaking the Bones, the Liver Flow, Sacrum Tapping, and the Heart Center Meditation. Weekly, use the Full-Body Energy Connection, Jaw Work, Eye Work, and Free-Form Energy Movement.

Surgery

After surgery, follow all of the recovery instructions from your surgeon, and give yourself extra rest and sleep to allow the body's self-healing mechanisms to do their magic. You may use both the Circular Breath and the Abdominal Breath to assist with the initial healing.

Surgery affects the energy body in two ways; first it is a shock to the system, often causing asustado afterward, as described in chapter 1. Secondly, the anesthetic can hang around for quite some time and affect the subtle body. Once you are able to be up and about, use Shaking the Bones very gently every day, as long as you are able to do so without interfering with the required surgical healing. Start very slowly, then add more time as your body allows. This practice will help with the asustado and also help clear the anesthetic. You may use the Full-Body Energy Connection daily as well.

You can add Toe Tapping into this regimen, depending on the surgery you had. **Do not use Toe Tapping after knee or hip surgery unless your surgeon has cleared you to do this movement.** Some surgeons may tell you to never again use Toe Tapping if you've had certain types of hip surgery. You can describe the movement to your surgeon, and he or she will tell you if it is OK.

TMJ

In addition to the following practices, you may want to see a TCM practitioner for acupuncture. Daily, use Free-Form Energy Movement, Jaw Work, Toe Tapping, and the Metta Meditation. Also use the yogic pigeon stretch.

Viral Illnesses

Common, short-lived viral illnesses—such as colds, influenza, upper and lower respiratory-tract infections, sinus infections, and gastroenteritis—must be monitored to ensure they do not become severe or that serious secondary bacterial infections don't develop. In addition, there are energy practices you can use to help the body move through the illness more quickly and to help prevent complications. You can also use a sequence of energy practices as a form of prevention when you travel or are in close contact with another person who is ill.

At the first sign of a viral illness, start by using Shaking the Bones for at least ten minutes to see if you can move the energy through your system more quickly. Next, use High-Heart Tapping, Back-of-the-Heart Tapping, and the Circular Breath. Continue by using the Toe Tapping for five minutes, and then return to Shaking the Bones for a few more minutes. Finally, use High-Heart Tapping and Back-of-the-Heart Tapping again. As time allows, continue to use these practices, plus the Full-Body Energy Connection, each day while you are experiencing the illness.

It's helpful to tap on the specific area in which you're having symptoms. For example, tap all over the chest for two to five minutes for chest symptoms such as coughing. Tap on the face and sinuses for two to five minutes for sinus symptoms, and tap gently all over the abdomen for five minutes for gastrointestinal symptoms.

Women's Reproductive Health

PMS and Menstruation

The discomfort of premenstrual syndrome (PMS) and menstruation primarily comes from a temporary inflammatory process in the pelvis, which is triggered when the cervix opens and sloughs off a layer of uterus. Daily, you can use gentle Full-Body Tapping, focusing on the belly, hips, and sacrum, and then use the pigeon stretch from yoga. In addition, Jaw Work can assist with keeping the hips open. You may use Connecting with the Earth if the pain is not responding to the practices, as it can help right away.

Fertility and Preparing for Pregnancy

Use all of the leg, hip, and pelvis exercises in this book to help prepare the pelvis for the pregnancy. You might especially work with High-Heart Tapping and the Liver Flow. Practice Full-Body Sensing, Connecting with the Earth, and Free-Form Energy Movement at least weekly.

Pregnancy

Do not use Toe Tapping during pregnancy, because it may stimulate the meridian points that activate labor. If you're using any of the other tapping practices, use Sacred Touch on your abdomen instead of tapping there. Otherwise, during pregnancy, you can use many of the other energy exercises. To begin with and most importantly, send energy to the baby through your belly using Sacred Touch as many times a day as you like. Practice the Circular Breath, Root Chakra Breath, and Abdominal Breath throughout the day as well. I also suggest the Heart Center Meditation and High-Heart Tapping daily. Weekly you may practice the Chakra Meditation, without the rapid breath. Try using Connecting to the Earth weekly; lie on your side once your belly is too large for you to lie on your stomach.

Menopause

Menopause is handled well with botanical medicine and TCM, and if it feels too difficult to handle, discuss estrogen supplementation with your primary-care practitioner. You may use the practices below as well.

Hot flashes are large influxes of energy. If you can manage them, you may learn to appreciate them for their energy infusion, and you may even find you enjoy them. You can also use Shaking the Bones while you're having a hot flash to move the extra energy through your body more quickly.

Another way to address hot flashes is to use a daily, thirty-minute energy practice that includes Toe Tapping, Shaking the Bones, or Full-Body Tapping—your choice—along with the Heart Center Meditation each morning. Also implement a daily exercise regimen to help the symptoms of menopause become more tolerable. Exercise moves energy quickly and effectively and this is important in menopause.

ENERGY HEALING TECHNIQUES FOR CHILDREN

Kids use energy exercises naturally. You may introduce the Toe Tapping and the Shaking the Bones practices to them. Toe Tapping is wonderful to help children with anxiety; they can quickly learn to manage and shift their emotions through this practice. Shaking the Bones is good for any time that children have excess energy or are just about to enter into a situation that requires them to sit still for a period of time. Have them try it for five to ten minutes, and play music for them while they do it.

The Abdominal Breath is a good breath practice for kids. To make it easy for children to understand this breath, have them visualize a balloon in their belly; guide them to blow up the balloon on each inhale and deflate the balloon with the exhale. The Abdominal Breath is good for relaxation or pain management, especially if they are about to undergo a medical or dental procedure.

A Final Story

I was in Mexico with a group of friends who were all devoted to experiencing the field of awareness and to the awake nature of energy. We had gone to Mexico to visit Maria Matus, the niece of Juan Matus, the shaman from the Carlos Castaneda novels. On the trip, we cultivated our connection to the larger field of energy and awareness, tracked energy and the field for learning, and shared dreams. Because we knew the journey was the destination, we paid attention to each and every aspect of our journey, not only whether or not we saw the healer and what she did with each of us.

One day, some women from the Seri tribe came to sell some of their wares at the house where we were staying. We bartered and talked with the women, and eventually we invited them inside. As we all sat at the big table in the kitchen, I dispensed coffee and food to all our Seri guests. All of us in our group were energy healers, and we began to use our hands to do healings on the women, as they seemed to need it and were open to it.

These women immediately "dropped in" to the presence, the connection to the field of awareness that we held, and began to tell their creation stories and personal stories in their own language. We knew what was happening; we were holding a field of love and healing strong enough that the Seri women were pulled into their own ceremony instinctively. They spoke in their Seri dialect and told stories, one by one. They cried and were somber and laughed as they told their lineage and stories. Our job was to listen and hold space. While there was no translation, we knew exactly what was happening.

While the women were visiting, Lydia, the Seri shaman with the group, mentioned to me that she felt the presence so strongly with our group. As they left, Lydia also commented on how strongly the women had felt their deity, the pelican, and how happy they were to be with us.

When we hold presence and awareness, healing pops up spontaneously. We cannot have a healing or learning experience that is separate from our energy body or the energy of the greater field of awareness around us. But through energy practices like those we've explored in this book and by following the flow of energy in the body, we can incorporate the wisdom of the field of awareness into our energy bodies, and from there it can heal our physical bodies.

When we change how energy is held in the body, we find that both our health and our experience of the world around us shift. The energy-healing journey takes us into the body and the heart. The energy of our body is our awakened guide into healing states, and the journey to these states is both long and enjoyable. We can practice the art of energy healing for years and years, and there will always be something new to learn and experience. Constant slow improvement, constant exploration of the energy in your body and the field of awareness around you, constant tracking of energy, constant listening and learning, will take you into places you could only have imagined.

NOTES AND ADDITIONAL REFERENCES

Chapter 1: The Basics of Energy Healing

1. Georg Feuerstein, *The Yoga Tradition: Its History, Literature, Philosophy, and Practice* (Prescott, AZ: Hohm Press, 1998), 123.

2. Alex Holland, *Voices of Qi: An Introductory Guide to Traditional Chinese Medicine* (Seattle: Northwest Institute of Acupuncture and Oriental Medicine, 1997), 75.

3. Pamela Miles and Gaia True, "Reiki—Review of a Biofield Therapy History, Theory, Practice, and Research," *Alternative Therapies in Health and Medicine* 9, no. 2 (March/April 2003), 62–72.

4. John S. Haller Jr., *Swedenborg, Mesmer, and the Mind/Body Connection: The Roots of Complementary Medicine* (West Chester, PA: Swedenborg Foundation, 2010), 72.

5. Erwin H. Ackerknecht, *Medicine at the Paris Hospital 1794–1848* (Baltimore: Johns Hopkins University Press, 1967), 53.

6. National Center for Complementary and Alternative Medicine (NCCAM), "Energy Medicine: An Overview," *Backgrounder* (National Institutes of Health, 2003).

7. Ibid.

8. Ibid.

9. Gary E. Schwartz, *The Energy Healing Experiments: Science Reveals Our Natural Power to Heal* (New York: Atria, 2007), 138–147.

10. Victoria Maizes and Tieraona Low Dog, eds., *Integrative Women's Health* (New York: Oxford University Press, 2010), 125–135.

11. Maureen Lockhart, *The Subtle Energy Body: The Complete Guide* (Rochester, VT: Inner Traditions, 2010), 89.

12. Peter Deadman and Mazin Al-Khafaji, *A Manual of Acupuncture* (East Sussex, UK: Journal of Chinese Medicine Publications, 2011), 11.

13. Feuerstein, 10.

14. Lockhart, 29.

15. Carlos Castaneda, *The Teachings of Don Juan: A Yaqui Way of Knowledge* (Berkeley: University of California Press, 1969), xvi. While there has been controversy about whether Don Juan Matus, the shaman featured in Castaneda's books, was real or a composite of shamans that Castaneda put together for his writings, I have met many people in Mexico who knew this *nagual* (shaman), and I have even met some of Don Juan's family members. Although Castaneda's books are considered novels, many of the healing details he describes match those I've learned in my work with Yaqui shamans. These Yaqui shamans confirmed that the healing knowledge was correct and that the characters in Castaneda's books are or were real members of their community.

16. It is possible my hands-on work stimulated a placebo response that helped her recover more quickly. If that is part of how energy healing works, I am thrilled. The placebo response is real; we call it *placebo* because we do not know what is responsible for the healing. Placebo response or an unexplained healing response accounts for up to 30 percent of healing. We want the placebo effect, and perhaps part of the placebo response is the effect of energy and mind-body medicine.

17. Schwartz, 125–127.

18. Herbert Benson, *The Relaxation Response* (New York: Harper Torch, 1975), 120–121.

Chapter 2: Connecting into the Unified Energy Field and the Shamanic Field

1. Bonnie Horrigan, "Shamanic Healing: We Are Not Alone—An Interview of Michael Harner," *Shamanism* 10, no. 1 (Spring/Summer 1997).

2. Ibid.

3. Ibid.

4. Castaneda, xvii.

5. Ibid.

Chapter 3: Getting Started: Using Movement to Open, Clear, Ground, and Receive Energy

1. Deadman and Al-Khafaji, 610–611.

2. James Asher, *Shaman Drums* (Sammasati Music, 2002).

Chapter 4: The Heart Center and the Art of Sacred Touch

1. The word *chorded* is from music and can apply to energy centers as well. When any two vibrations are chorded or used together, they influence each other. In music, it means that when two or three or four strings of an instrument are played at once they create a new and additional sound through harmonics. This is how I see healing and the heart center, or any organ or other chakra or dan tien: used together, they create harmonies and an overtone or new vibration. I use *chord* instead of *cord*, or tied, as there is a different meaning in a vibrational sense. One energy influences the other.
2. Doc Childre and Howard Martin, *The HeartMath Solution* (New York: HarperCollins, 1999), 34. This book describes a wonderful body of work, and if you are interested in this work, I highly recommend reading it.
3. Ibid.
4. Ibid.
5. Karunesh, *Heart Chakra Meditation* (Oreade Music, 2003).

Chapter 5: Sensing and Moving Energy

1. Lockhart, 37.
2. W. Brugh Joy, *Joy's Way: A Map for the Transformational Journey* (Los Angeles: J. P. Tarcher, 1979), 269.
3. A simple rattle can be made by putting dried seeds, corn, or beans in a can or plastic container. First, open the top of an aluminum can and leave the top attached at one place. After you empty, clean, and dry the can, place the dried seeds, corn, or beans in it and fasten the lid closed with strong tape. If you like, you can also poke a hole into the unopened end of the can and secure a stick or handle there.

   A plastic container with a lid (such as a vitamin bottle) can also be used to make a quick, simple rattle. A wooden box or cup also makes a nice rattle with a lovely sound. Test the rattle once you make it (or before you buy it) to see if it feels good and if you are happy with the way it moves energy. Each rattle is different; find one or make one that you like.

Chapter 6: Balance, Alignment, and Body Wisdom

1. *The Random House Dictionary* (New York: Random House, 1967), 112.
2. "Balance," *Merriam-Webster.com*, 2012.

3. Karina Stewart, LAc, DOM, personal communication, March 2002.
4. Anugama, "The Chakra Journey," *Shamanic Dream* (Open Sky Music, 2002).
5. If you want more breathwork, I suggest you practice with the *Ananda Mandala* meditation by Sri Krishnaraj, available as a CD or mp3 download by the same name (Kosmic Music US, 2008). This is a wonderful chakra meditation, but be warned that it is a difficult one.

Chapter 7: Specific Energy Centers and Targeted Energy-Movement Techniques

1. Castaneda, xvii.
2. Deadman and Al-Khafaji, 572, 602.
3. Clinton Ober, Stephen T. Sinatra, and Martin Zucker, *Earthing: The Most Important Health Discovery Ever?* (Laguna Beach, CA: Basic Health Publications, 2010), 20.
4. Deadman and Al-Khafaji, 17, 591.

Chapter 8: Receptivity

1. Castaneda, xv.

Additional References

Brennan, Barbara Ann. *Hands of Light: A Guide to Healing through the Human Energy Field.* New York: Bantam, 1988.
_____. *Light Emerging: The Journey of Personal Healing.* New York: Bantam, 1993.
Bruyere, Rosalyn. *Wheels of Light: Chakras, Auras, and the Healing Energy of the Body.* New York: Fireside, 1994.
Co, Master Stephen, and Eric B. Robins. *The Power of Prana.* Boulder, CO: Sounds True, 2011.
Dahn Yoga Education. *Dahn Yoga Basics.* Sedona, AZ: Healing Society, 2006.
Maciocia, Giovanni. *The Foundations of Chinese Medicine: A Comprehensive Text for Acupuncturists and Herbalists,* 2nd ed. London: Elsevier, 2005.
Mehl-Madrona, Lewis. *Narrative Medicine: The Use of History and Story in the Healing Process.* Rochester, VT: Bear and Company, 2007.
Porta, Miquel, ed. *A Dictionary of Epidemiology,* 5th ed. New York: Oxford University Press, 2008.

ACKNOWLEDGMENTS

I would like to thank my teachers Maria Elena Cairo and the late W. Brugh Joy, MD, for their wonderful teachings on energy, awareness, and presence. I would also like to acknowledge Karina Stewart, DOM, for her wonderful initiatory teachings on toe tapping, shaking the bones, and body tapping.

Heart Chakra Meditation — Kamuesh

Shaman Drums — James Asher

"Amour" (song)

ABOUT THE AUTHOR

Ann Marie Chiasson, MD, MPH, CCFP, is Canadian Board certified in family practice and completed a fellowship in Integrative Medicine through Dr. Andrew Weil's Arizona Center for Integrative Medicine. She has extensive experience exploring energy medicine and alternative healing practices, having trained with Dr. Brugh Joy and Maria Elena Cairo, as well as other shamanic healers and psychic surgeons. Currently, she has a private integrative and energy healing practice in Tucson, where she offers consultations, treatments, seminars, and retreats. She also teaches through the Arizona Center for Integrative Medicine and facilitates spirituality and healing conferences. For more information, please visit annmariechiassonmd.com and handsturnedon.com.